T0008339

The MODERN WITCHCRAFT Book of Crystal Magick

YOUR COMPLETE GUIDE TO THE *Power of Crystals*

Judy Ann Nock

Author of *The Modern Witchcraft Guide to Magickal Herbs*

Adams Media

New York London Toronto Sydney New Delhi

DEDICATION

To Jaime, my gem, my treasure.

Adams Media
An Imprint of Simon & Schuster, Inc.
100 Technology Center Drive
Stoughton, Massachusetts 02072

First Adams Media hardcover edition September 2023

For information about special discounts for bulk purchases, please contact Simon & Schuster Special Sales at 1-866-506-1949 or business@simonandschuster.com.

The Simon & Schuster Speakers Bureau can bring authors to your live event. For more information or to book an event, contact the Simon & Schuster Speakers Bureau at 1-866-248-3049 or visit our website at www.simonspeakers.com.

Interior design by Colleen Cunningham
Interior images © 123RF; Getty Images; Simon & Schuster, Inc.

Manufactured in the United States of America

10 9 8 7 6 5 4 3 2 1

Library of Congress Cataloging-in-Publication Data has been applied for.

ISBN 978-1-5072-2118-1
ISBN 978-1-5072-2119-8 (ebook)

This book is intended as general information only, and should not be used to diagnose or treat any health condition. In light of the complex, individual, and specific nature of health problems, this book is not intended to replace professional medical advice. The ideas, procedures, and suggestions in this book are intended to supplement, not replace, the advice of a trained medical professional. Consult your physician before adopting any of the suggestions in this book, as well as about any condition that may require diagnosis or medical attention. The author and publisher disclaim any liability arising directly or indirectly from the use of this book.

Acknowledgments

I would like to acknowledge my agent, June Clark, and my editors, Rebecca Tarr and Brett Palana-Shanahan, for helping make this book a reality. I would like to thank the following institutions for accommodating my research: the Gemological Institute of America; the American Museum of Natural History, especially George Harlow, Curator Emeritus of Mineralogy; and the New York Public Library. I would also like to thank the Metropolitan Museum of Art for their support. I am forever grateful for the support of my family, including my parents, James and Bonnie Nock; my siblings, Teri and Robert Nock; my extended family, including Darra Zankman, Cindy and John Nock, Ben and Samantha Nock, Jessica Paniagua, and Mary Nock; as well as my friends, including Dr. Ann Gaba, Stephanie Ritchie, Rick Kariolic, Leigh Brown, Debby Schwartz, Shaula Chambliss, Dena Moes, Barbara McGlamery, Melissa Whitehead, Amanda Sullivan, Donna Distefano, Tim Jensen, Julie Gillis, Gretchen Sosnowski, Elohim Leafar, Sumru Aricanli, and David Kizirian. I appreciate and thank all of the talented musicians I have had the privilege to share many stages with this year, especially Debby Schwartz, Andrew Gilchrist, Louie Zhelesnik, Chuck Tumulty, and Ivan Julian, James Mastro, Al Maddy, Jared Michael Nickerson, Stephen Goulding, and Mike Ratti. I want to acknowledge and thank Geraldine Beskin and The Atlantis Bookshop, Marya Banu of the Metropolitan Museum of Art Museum Store, and Elizabeth Herrera and Kristina Sanchez of Barnes & Noble for their continued support. I especially want to express my deep gratitude to my readers. Thank you for staying with me all these years.

Contents

PART TWO
A LIBRARY OF CRYSTALS 61

PART THREE
HOW TO USE CRYSTALS IN MAGICK 119

Introduction

Imagine holding a magickal tool formed hundreds of thousands of years ago. Born in the veins of the earth, it carries the energy of the vast expanse of geologic time, of the very memory of the earth, of all that is eternal.

This is your crystal.

The enchantment of crystals is at your fingertips, and their vibrational energies are yours to explore, whether you wish to create balance or invite healing. Crystals enchant, inspire, and enhance the magickal practice of the modern witch like no other tool of the craft. From tumbled stones to crystal points, clusters, slices, and spheres, *The Modern Witchcraft Book of Crystal Magick* is the comprehensive book you need to gain a deep understanding of crystals and how to use them to elevate your craft and expand your practice.

In this book, you'll learn how to identify mineral types and their metaphysical attributes and how to incorporate crystals into your magick. You'll also find a library of fifty-five crystals with their magickal properties and associations so you can choose the perfect one for spellcasting. Used properly in divination, meditation, spells, charms, jewelry, and talismans, these gifts from the earth never cease to capture and transform the imagination. Crystals have so much appeal due to their inherent qualities that have the potential to open hearts and expand minds. Even people new to the craft or those who are just intrigued by crystals and want to learn more will enjoy discovering how crystals are formed and why various powers are attributed to them.

For modern witchcraft, crystals are powerful tools for divination, energy work, and change. Your crystal is your conduit, a channel through which your mind may be opened to its higher power. It can lead you to a place of peace, help you tap into your psychic abilities, and allow for transformation to occur. Crystals allow you to grow in harmonic resonance to your surroundings and reflect your spiritual awakening in something tangible. Unlock the magick of crystals and experience the timeless beauty, power, and wisdom of the earth!

PART ONE

AN OVERVIEW OF CRYSTALS

In this first part you will learn the historical and scientific fundamentals behind the magick of crystals and understand how these ancient and powerful gifts from the earth became integral to modern witchcraft. You'll learn about the physicality of crystals, such as the different shapes and colors they can be found in, as well as magickal patterns of light and other crystal inclusions that can be found. As you explore this part, you'll also learn about how to choose the right crystals for you and your magickal workings and how to cleanse, clear, charge, and store your crystals.

Through understanding the inherent qualities that make crystals so captivating and collectible, you will discover ways to supercharge your witchcraft as you gain wisdom from the earth. Using crystals as working magickal tools has no downsides. Doing so will only enhance your witchcraft. Crystals connect you to heaven and earth, to the past and the future, to the hidden realms of magick and the observable majesty of the earth mother. Use them with joy. Use them with respect. Use them with love. Use them well.

Chapter 1

MAGICK and CRYSTALS

If you find that you have an affinity for attuning to the earth, if you already practice natural magick and enjoy expressing yourself through spells and rituals, or if you like intentional arrangements of your environment to reflect that which you seek to manifest, then you may be a crystal witch. Crystals can evoke feelings of peace and well-being, absorb light or break it into patterns, and aid in transcendence, all of which make them a natural fit for the modern practice of witchcraft.

In this chapter, you will learn about the nature of crystals, how different crystals reflect and capture light, and how those connections can affect the energy you can use them for. You'll also learn about the inclusions (bubbles or streaks, for example) in some crystals and how those visual differences can change how you interact with crystals in your magick. Finally, you'll learn to respect where your crystals come from and why you should rid them of any negative energy from mishandling.

THE PATH OF THE CRYSTAL WITCH

Why should a modern witch use crystals? The answer is multifaceted. Incorporating crystals into your witchcraft is a type of natural magick. Crystals are remarkably powerful because they are composed of elements joined together by the forces of nature. Natural crystals get their color and shape from the trace elements present during their formation and from the tremendous amount of heat and pressure in their subterranean environment. This makes them inherently magickal for witches, as they embody elemental intensity, representing the union of earth, air, fire, and water.

In addition, crystals have been used to focus, reflect, absorb, and direct energy. This is useful especially in spellcasting. In spellcasting, a witch will set an intention and raise energy to empower that intention in order to call it into being. Crystals are frequently used as tools to aid and amplify this work. In fact, some witch's tools are directly made from crystals.

The minerals and elements that crystals are composed of have been found everywhere from microscopic organisms to the human body and even in the stars. Witches know that this displays how everything is connected—from the tiniest living beings to celestial objects. When you explore these connections, you are able to use them to enhance your practice. By exploring the origins of crystals, you delve into a deep understanding of your observable reality. This understanding can help you unlock the things you cannot see, such as the delicate threads of magick and fate that you weave, interpret, alter, and otherwise influence.

Finally, it should be noted that some crystals have the observable ability to call things to themselves. This power of attraction is also intuitively felt and is the basic tenet of certain types of manifestation magick. Attraction in magick deals with the things you wish to call unto yourself and using crystals that possess natural magnetism is an excellent way to enhance spells of attraction.

CRYSTAL FORMATION

Before you start using crystals in a supernatural way, it is worth exploring the events and sequences that inform their natural way of being. Crystals have the ability to exhibit magickal properties, unique energy signatures, and vibrational frequencies. Understanding how they are formed will add depth and specificity to your craft.

The process of crystallization is a three-stage reordering of molecular elements from a chaotic arrangement to an ordered one. The process is inherently magickal because it represents the union of all the elements: earth, air, fire, and water. Crystallization begins with nucleation—when elemental atoms or molecules first encounter each other. This encounter is usually triggered by a gas vapor or a melt, but crystallization usually happens in one of three ways. Melted rock, or magma, contains a lot of kinetic energy and as it cools, atoms encounter each other and begin to form crystals. Crystallization can also begin through chemical reactions and in the presence of water. These encounters occur in pockets within layers of the earth. These pockets are often hollow chambers where temperatures and internal pressure are very high. After the elements encounter one another, either as a part of melted rock, or dissolved in water, or in a gas vapor, the growth stage is activated. This growth stage represents the rendering of chaos into order as crystals follow a repeated pattern of growth to form clusters and points, and sometimes aggregates, which is when different types of crystals form side by side. Finally, the last stage is termination, where the growth stops. Crystal growth can be stopped by a change in temperature, a change in pressure, or space limitations. There really aren't any restrictions other than environmental ones that can limit how large a crystal can grow. If conditions remain constant and space is not an issue, it is conceivable that a crystal can continue to grow indefinitely.

CRYSTALLOGRAPHY BASICS

For a witch working with crystals, it is often helpful to know a bit about crystal forms and structures—a branch of science known as crystallography. While it is useful to understand basic crystallography, a lot of crystals that you encounter might not appear as they are described here because they are smaller parts of larger crystals that have been mined. The patterns begin at the molecular level and they repeat and repeat, but you might not always notice them, particularly if the crystal's individual units are small, or it has been tumbled, cut, or polished. However, it is still important to know about them.

Crystals follow repeating patterns that are symmetrical and this symmetrical repetition of individual units forms a lattice. A lattice is a repeated structure, and these structures will have three or four axes and can be rotated so that the symmetry shows three, four, or six faces. The naturally occurring symmetry of crystals has an interesting alignment with some of the core elements of witchcraft. Patterns such as three, four, and six are considered useful in magick. For instance, some witches follow the Law of Three, where magick that is done returns to the witch threefold whether it is good or bad. Some witches worship the triple goddess, and many witches work with the four elements and the four directions. And six is three doubled, and is considered auspicious for that reason.

There are seven different crystal systems from which crystals get their lattice structure:

- **Cubic:** the most symmetrical of the seven systems; crystals form at right angles of equal length. Isometric is another name for the cubic system and their meaning is equivalent. The cubic system has total symmetry. Fluorite, garnet, and pyrite are examples of crystals with cubic symmetry. Cubic crystals are useful during points of balance, such as the fall and spring equinoxes, which are celebrated by many witches as the sabbats of Mabon and Ostara, respectively.
- **Hexagonal:** the rarest of the seven systems; some examples include six-sided prisms and double-sided pyramids. The hexagonal crystal system has four axes: Three are horizontal and equal in length, while the vertical axis can be longer or shorter than the other three. This gives the unit a honeycomb cross section. (Honey is frequently used in witchcraft as a sacred offering, and the "bee priestesses" [called the Melissae] of ancient Greece were believed to possess the power of prophecy.) Apatite, aquamarine, and golden beryl are examples of crystals with hexagonal symmetry. For this reason, they can be used as altar offerings or for divination purposes by connecting how their sacred form repeats in different aspects of nature.
- **Monoclinic:** the most common of the seven crystal systems; the axes are not equal in length and the lattice resembles orderly stacking blocks. There are three axes, and two are perpendicular to each other and one slants. Monoclinic crystals span a huge range of magickal applications because there are so many of them, including malachite, azurite, charoite, jade, selenite, and moonstone.
- **Orthorhombic:** Orthorhombic crystals have a twofold symmetry, which means you can rotate the crystal 180 degrees and it won't change its appearance. Any two edges can be right angles, but they do

not have to be the same length. This 180-degree symmetry is magickally significant because polarity is a guiding factor in witchcraft. Equal opposites such as goddess and god, night and day, full moon and new moon are considered to be powerful entities to work with and auspicious times for certain types of spells. Orthorhombic crystals such as iolite, celestite, and peridot are useful for balance, ascension, and healing, respectively.

- **Tetragonal:** Tetragonal crystals have fourfold symmetry, so they won't appear to change appearance after a 90-degree rotation. The tetragonal system also has three axes and is similar to the cubic system, only the vertical axis is longer, giving the crystals an elongated appearance when compared to cubic crystals. Think of this elongation as an expansion or a stretch. Tetragonal crystals may call you to ascend or reach for new abilities and heights. Apophyllite and wulfenite are examples of tetragonal crystals, and they are both useful for connecting with higher planes.
- **Triclinic:** All three axes are unequal in length and the angles aren't perpendicular to each other. These crystals have only one axis of symmetry. This means that it is possible in only one place for a line you envision entering the crystal unit to be able to exit at about what would appear to be the same point on an opposite side. Every other axis is going to be at a slanted angle. The triclinic system reminds you to be at the center of your craft. In witchcraft, grounding and centering is an important tenet of spellcasting. This is because witches work with mysterious and powerful energies that can seem to come from all sides: above, below, within, or from any external direction. This makes triclinic crystals useful for manifesting, channeling, and protection. In these types of magick, you place yourself at the center. Labradorite and amazonite are triclinic crystals used for protective magick, while sunstone and aventurine are triclinic crystals used for manifesting prosperity.
- **Trigonal:** Also called rhombohedral, the trigonal system is generally considered to be a subsystem of the hexagonal system because the crystals have four axes of equal length and threefold symmetry, which means you can rotate them 120 degrees and they will look the same as they did in the starting position. Trigonal crystals resemble cubic crystals that have been skewed a bit, which creates six parallel faces. Many of the most widely used crystals in witchcraft such as clear quartz,

amethyst, and citrine are all trigonal crystals. They are distinct for many reasons but are especially recognizable in their natural form of clusters that terminate in a pyramid. Pyramids are symbols of eternity and were built to glorify the life after death. Trigonal crystals connect you to the spiritual realms by serving as powerful reminders of the continuation of energy beyond what you can perceive.

In addition, some of the crystals you will encounter will not fit into these crystal systems and are considered amorphous. For example, jet is not technically a crystal but a type of petrified wood, obsidian is actually a type of glass, and opal takes on the crystal structure of other minerals and doesn't have a lattice pattern of its own. They may look like crystals, carry energy like crystals, and are effective to use in magick like crystals, but their structure doesn't have a repeating pattern.

Some crystals that follow the repeated patterns of their system will have individual unit cells that are so small, they can't be seen without magnification. This is why some crystals will have a very distinct form, but some won't. For example, clear quartz will look like a six-sided prism topped with a little pyramid, but other varieties of quartz like amethyst grow in tight clusters and all you see is the pointed pyramid top. And a lot of crystals will follow the pattern of their system, but their individual crystals are so small that you need a microscope to see them (microcrystalline) or that even with magnification, you really can't see them at all (cryptocrystalline). So, they won't look like the classic prism or pyramid shape that a lot of people associate with crystals, but the pattern is still there even if the mineral just looks like a giant slab. Magickally, this can remind you that small actions and rituals can make a big impact and that there is beauty and power in repetition whether as part of a formal rite or a tiny wish.

THE INTERACTION OF CRYSTALS AND LIGHT

Crystals attract your eye because of what they are able to do with light. Light is a form of energy, and by understanding how crystals and light interact you can begin to understand their influence on other more subtle types of energy. In witchcraft, energy is often manipulated in order to achieve a goal or bring about change. Understanding the way crystals interact with light can help you identify powerful ways to use them.

Here are some of the most common optical properties of crystals:

- **Crystals of Light: Transparency.**
  Transparency describes how light passes through a crystal and how the light can be distributed or scattered by the crystal. For example, quartz crystal is clear and completely transparent, meaning that you can see clear through it and can easily make out objects behind the crystal. Transparent crystals can be used to attain mental clarity.

- **Dark Crystals: Opacity.**
  Opaque crystals absorb light to the extent that you cannot see through them at all. Opaque crystals do not allow light to pass through, but they do reflect light back to your eye. You interpret this reflected light as a color. An opaque crystal that absorbs light can also be used to absorb negative energy. Onyx is a good example of an opaque crystal.

- **Crystals That Shine: Metallic.**
  Metallic crystals have a unique luster that is generally accepted to be an attractive characteristic. Metallic crystals reflect light and have a sheen that has the appearance of metal on their surface, as the name suggests. Metallic crystals can be used as wards: They can reflect things away from you and are useful in protection magic or to stave off an undesired outcome. Galena is one type of metallic crystal. Metallic crystals are always opaque and are usually the color of metal: silver, gold, or copper. Pyrite is a metallic crystal that resembles gold.

- **Rainbow Crystals: Iridescence.**
  Iridescence is a play of color exhibited by crystals that are able to break white light up into its spectral colors and reflect those colors back to you, either on the surface or internally. Some crystals will have an internal iridescence where a rainbow effect can be seen within the crystal. Other types of crystals such as labradorite will have an iridescent surface. Fire agates can show iridescence just below the surface. Iridescent crystals are useful in complex magic or when internal emotional work is required.

- **Crystals That Glow: Adularescence.**
  Some crystals such as moonstone appear to have a bluish or white floating light that moves just beneath the surface. This effect, adularescence, is caused by light interacting inside of the crystal. Light enters

the stone and then is reflected off of internal molecular surfaces, making it look like the stone is glowing from within. The glow will move as the crystal is handled or rotated. Adularescent crystals are excellent for spiritual work such as divination, calling upon ancestors and angels, and meditation.

- **Crystal "Eyes": Chatoyancy.**
  Crystals that are polished with a smooth rounded surface may have internal characteristics that create a glowing band of light across the surface. These very thin, needlelike inclusions, called "silks" due to their fine nature, interact with light in a unique way, making it appear that a band of light is moving across the surface of the crystal. Chatoyant crystals can be used to attune with familiars. The banded light is universally accepted to resemble the eye of a cat, whose pupils will reduce to slits when exposed to light. These crystals are also useful for developing psychic sight and honing a witch's instincts and intuition. Tiger's eye and chrysoberyl are good examples of crystals that exhibit chatoyancy. Chatoyancy is often called the "cat's eye" effect.

CRYSTAL INCLUSIONS

In addition to the many ways crystals can reflect, absorb, refract, and transmit light, crystals also have unique internal characteristics called inclusions. Often referred to as "nature's fingerprints," inclusions are naturally occurring identifying characteristics that are present within the crystal lattice. Natural inclusions are often referred to as "jardin" (French for "garden"), or as "garden," because the internal world of crystals can appear like a world within a world with inclusions that can resemble things in nature such as moss, trees, and even rainbows. Inclusions can be caused by many different things such as water droplets that get trapped inside a crystal while it is forming or a trace element that will have an effect on the transparency of a crystal. Inclusions can also be indicators of a crystal's origin because some inclusions are commonly seen in specific geographic areas.

Crystal inclusions give an inner life and a distinct personality to each specimen. Inclusions can even help you identify the geographical origins of crystals, which can strengthen the bond between a crystal and a witch, particularly if a witch has a cultural or ancestral attachment to a specific geographic crystal-bearing region.

Here are common crystal inclusions and what they represent:

- **Bubbles:** Sometimes you will look inside your crystal and see a clear round or slightly tapered shape. A bubble inclusion in a crystal can mean that this crystal will help you connect with a deeply held secret or something that you wish to protect.
- **Lily pads:** Lily pads, named for their appearance, are caused by tiny crystals growing inside of crystals. Peridot will often show a lily pad inclusion. These crystals within crystals, particularly when they occur in peridot, symbolize growth in a relationship. Lily pad inclusions have a distinct oval appearance.
- **Garden scenes:** Emeralds are the most famous crystals for internal gardens. These are networks of crystals within crystals that are naturally growing inside and can vary in appearance, size, and location, giving the crystal what appears to be an inner landscape. Sometimes if they reach the surface, they can appear as chips or cracks, so it is important to know that not every crystal with an internal garden and an inclusion that reaches the surface is damaged. As you develop an eye for inclusions, you will be able to tell the difference between natural inclusions and damage. Teaching yourself how to use magnification helps a lot. A crystal with a rich garden is useful in magick that deals with balancing the emotions and emotional healing and growth.
- **Rutile:** Rutile is a type of mineral that occurs in a lot of crystals and usually appears as a thin, needle-like structure. Rutiles are iridescent "melt relics" deep within a crystal. Embedded in the crystal lattice, rutiles (also called "silks") can create a dazzling array of effects depending on how they line up. They can create star effects, internal webs, and all manner of natural beauty. Crystals with rutiles symbolize complexity and are well suited to advanced magick and pathworking.
- **"Negative" crystals:** These types of inclusions do not represent negative energy, but rather they are symbolic of the unknown. Excellent for magickal seeking spells such as finding a lost item or establishing contact with a spirit, a negative crystal inclusion can appear as a shadow of where a crystal once was or as a cubic growth on the surface. Sometimes it will be on the surface if a crystal was part of a cluster and some of the cluster has cleaved off, leaving a damage-free mark of where it

used to be. It has a different appearance than a chip or a crack. Instead it will look like an impression of a crystal and have a symmetrical silhouette. Or the negative crystal can be seen inside the crystal itself, symbolizing spirit or soul energy. If you see a negative crystal on the surface of a crystal, you can use it for different types of magick, particularly in releasing spells and healing spells. Negative crystal inclusions can serve as tangible proof that separation can be endured and that beauty does remain.

- **Rainbow inclusions:** Sometimes crystals will exhibit an internal cleavage line or what appears to be a crack. When the crystal is rotated, a spectrum of color can be seen. In magick, rainbow inclusions are considered auspicious because they represent attainment, fulfillment, and peace.
- **Dendritic inclusions:** Dendritic inclusions, often caused by iron oxides, are among the most beautiful and mysterious internal inclusions. They appear as tiny trees or roots and look like miniature worlds growing inside of the crystal. These crystals are potent for manifesting desires. Dendritic inclusions are often seen in agates, amber, quartz crystals, and even some beryl group crystals such as aquamarine and emerald.

Take your time to observe and interact with your crystal's characteristics. When you discover a rainbow inclusion, this can be an indicator that something wonderful is on its way to you. The feeling of handling the receptive power of an opaque crystal is a different feeling from viewing the reflective beauty of a transparent crystal. You can use your crystals to draw things toward you or reflect them away. Iridescent crystals can inspire you and spark your inner fire. A crystal with an internal garden can put you in touch with your own internal emotional landscape. You may already have several crystals in your possession, and you should feel free to experience them in this new way. Get to know their unique properties and understand what makes them so special as you continue to learn about their extremely ancient and very complicated origins.

KNOW WHERE YOUR CRYSTALS COME FROM

Crystals have been found on every continent except Antarctica. When you think about the magickal implications of geologic time and how ancient the earth truly is, crystals simply do not adhere to our mundane understanding of time, much less the borders and boundaries of geography. Crystals sometimes get caught up in geopolitical turmoil because a discovery of desirable stones will stimulate the economy, leading to a rush to uncover as much as possible. Crystal formation is based in geology, not geography, and when crystal deposits overlap the borders of competing countries, it is not uncommon for conflict to result.

As a witch, you will want to cleanse your crystals of any residual chaotic energy they may have been exposed to. (You can learn more about this in Chapter 3.) In some sense, any crystal is always representative of abundance just by its nature of being discovered. But this discovery comes at a cost. While many crystals are revealed through the natural processes of the earth such as erosion, others are extracted. Mineral-bearing earth, also known as ore, has two levels: The upper level contains oxide zones and carbonite zones while the lower level contains sulfide zones. The oxide zones are mineral bearing—this is where you find crystals such as rhodochrosite, malachite, and fluorite. And once these crystals become visible, they are exploited until it becomes unlikely that any more will be found. The demand for crystals, minerals, and gems always seems to be greater than the supply. Crystal mining can be small-scale and artisanal, but it can also be destructive and violent. Explosions and hazardous chemicals are commonplace in the mining process. The best way to avoid participating in this destruction is to always inquire about origin when buying crystals and to support small-scale sellers.

Where to Purchase Ethically Sourced Crystals

Many people who exhibit at gem and mineral shows are small-scale low-impact miners. Independently owned shops are often a good bet because they tend to know their vendors personally.

Learning the origins of your crystals will strengthen your relationships with them. A crystal uncovered in a violent or destructive fashion will need an energetic healing of its own. When you envision the distant locations of the geographic origins of crystals, you have to consider that many crystals formed long before our most distant ancestors had their fleeting span upon the earth. Think about where they have come from, how they were extracted, and how far they traveled through distance and time to grace your sacred space. And now that you have them, you owe it to yourself to learn how to use them to their fullest. Much more than aesthetic decor, crystals are magickal tools.

Chapter 2

WORKING with CRYSTAL MAGICK

Crystals are magick made visible. From the planets of the solar system to the aura of your body, crystals are an intrinsic part of an energy field that transcends space and time while influencing your material world in the present. Using crystals can help you attune to your core being and your desired outward manifestations. Now that you understand the origin of crystals, you are ready to discover more about the magick behind how they work. In this chapter, you will learn about the magickal systems of belief that explain the power of crystals. You will take a deep dive into the traditions of sympathetic magick and gain understanding of color theory and how it affects both magick and the mind. This knowledge will lead you to choose the crystals that resonate most strongly with your practice.

You'll also learn about the philosophy of animism, the tenets of contagious magick and sympathetic magick, how "like attracts like," as well as some of the cultural associations that many people have with crystals. In addition to learning about different magickal belief systems, you will also learn how the different shapes and colors of crystals impact their use and how to start using correspondences to create a basis for crystal spellcraft.

CRYSTALS AND ANIMISM

Just as people are widely thought of as physical beings inhabited by a soul, animism is a philosophy that recognizes that all natural objects have a sort of consciousness and that spiritual beings can and do affect the physical world. Natural magick, which crystals are an important part of, operates on two central doctrines: one having to do with souls or spirits that are incarnate (have physical forms) and the other having to do with spirits, apparitions, or ghosts that are discarnate (do not have physical forms). Biology can explain many aspects of life, death, illness, health, sleep, and dreams, but it doesn't explain trance, visions, passion, love, or shadow (the dark and often unexplored realms of the psyche). Natural magick is not new. It has been a practice of human beings across the ages. Beliefs have evolved and changed over time, but the connection between the natural world and the mage, or witch, has remained. The concept of spirit, a transcendent life force that defies the constructs of time and physicality, remains a steady line across many civilizations.

The discovery of crystals and minerals often coincided with the rise of early civilizations. Babylonians adorned their temples with lapis lazuli. Egyptians practiced alluvial mining along the Nile River. The cataloging of stones in ancient Greece is well documented. All of these societies also recognized the presence of a spirit inhabiting the body and a pantheon of gods that explained natural phenomena such as the flooding of rivers, the positions of stars, and the changing of seasons. Even in comparatively simple societies (groups of people that did not have a formal central government or established trade routes, or had nomadic or insular subsistent existences), ideas of spirit persisted, and they still do today.

In folklore and in poetry, ideas about the soul and the heart are plentiful. So too is the concept of a stone or crystal as a receptacle of power. In many Indigenous cultures, inanimate objects are acknowledged as possessing a living spirit. Rivers, trees, and stones are revered and even spoken to. They are respected and consulted as a personification of spiritual energy. Witches who work with crystals will often abide by the tenets of natural magick, which allow an external object such as a crystal to receive a transference of energy and therefore become imbued with power. The energy or force (the intention and will of the witch) will animate the object (the crystal) and turn it into a visible and tactile form of consciousness that is essentially an extension of the witch's own. By examining the historical and cultural foundations of natural magick, you can integrate the practices that strongly resonate with your desires and beliefs. Understanding and acknowledging origins, whether they are cultural, geographic, or geologic, will amplify your abilities to use crystals in magick.

CONTAGIOUS MAGICK AND CRYSTALS

Contagious magick is guided by the principle that objects and entities have the ability to act upon each other. Contagious magick is connected to animism in that the state of being organic or alive is not a requirement for anything to retain spirit or magickal potential. Only certain kinds of crystals, such as amber, are organic, but when a witch wields crystal magick, the magick animates the inanimate, using the natural abilities of the crystal to absorb, transfer, reflect, conduct, or otherwise transform spiritual essence. This potentiality is present in all crystals. Contagious magick gets its power from the fact that there is power in objects such as crystals and that this power can be moved from person to object and from object to person through connections made by proximity. These movements or transformations can be made in many ways, such as through touch and sight. Holding a crystal and looking through it are two ways to imbue it with power.

Contagious magick is indelibly linked to the sensuousness of being. A touch is electric: Impulses are sent externally through contact and travel internally to the brain. These pathways are strengthened with every repetition. This is why magick is considered a *practice*. In practicing witchcraft, you are conducting energy and creating these pathways. The more you practice them, the stronger they will get. The power of touch cannot be overstated. A touch is a link: Touch creates a connection between the crystal and the witch. There are myriad varieties of touch, and each one has a subtle energy signature of its own. Be mindful about how you handle your crystals and you will widen your abilities to imbue them with very specific kinds of power. Notice the discrete differences in modes of touch. Enclosing a crystal in your hand is a protective gesture, while caressing it with your fingertip has an entirely different purpose and feel, like how a kiss is different from a grasp. Explore the many ways that the energy of touch can be experienced and transferred and you will find yourself growing in your ability to explore the law of contact.

The Law of Contact

Witches, shamans, priests, and priestesses across many lands and many eras, including the present era, have used and continue to use the law of contact as a central principle of spellcasting. The effect of the law of contact was succinctly described by Sir James George Frazer in *The Golden Bough* (1890) as "things which have once been in contact with one another continue to act upon each other at a distance after the physical contact has been severed." This explains why witches use things such as hair or fingernails in some spells: They retain the essence of a person.

Witches interact with crystals in a physical way—through touch. This means that crystals can be used according to the law of contact. Crystals are both conductive and receptive. Just as energy can be transferred from a witch to a crystal, the crystal can also be used as a vehicle to remove burdens or unwanted energy. A crystal can also be imbued with a specific intention. One of the wonderful things about using crystals according to the law of contact is that intention is the driving force behind the magick. Touching a crystal will imbue it with your energy signature, and any subsequent contact with other elements will have a culminating or transferring effect on the energy that the crystal contains. You can also clear a crystal of residual energy and dedicate it anew. Crystals are infinitely recyclable as magickal tools. You may find that the more you use a particular crystal, the more adept you become at releasing, transforming, and manifesting desired outcomes.

You may also dedicate certain crystals for very specific purposes. For example, using a polished black onyx slab exclusively for divination will enhance your divination powers because you are touching it only for that purpose and it will reflect back to you only the accumulated energy that you have put into it.

The law of contact also allows you to work magick for other people. If you are asked for help revealing or resolving a situation for a friend, you can use their energy signature by incorporating crystals into the spell if you allow them to touch or carry around the crystal first. You may find that using crystals by the law of contact enhances your other powers of divination. If you were to do a tarot reading for someone, having them hold a crystal and then placing the crystal on top of the deck would amplify the query because the crystal acts as a conductor among the querent (the person requesting the reading), the oracle (the cards themselves), and the diviner (the person interpreting the reading). You can even use this method on your own if you are reading yourself; the crystal will aid in communicating your query with clarity.

Crystals can be used to link people and places as well. For example, if you are seeking a new job or admission to a new school, holding, touching, and carrying the crystal (allowing it to touch nothing else during this time) and then placing it in the auspicious location is a powerful part of manifesting magick. You have "placed" yourself, your energy signature, in the exact location where you wish to be. Crystals can also be used to link people if both people have touched the same crystal with the same intention. When you use crystals in this way, it is very important to practice ethics in the law of contact. Do not give a crystal to a person without telling them why and then ask for it back and try to work magick on them. Acknowledging consent and acting with honesty are core values, and manipulative magick, such as a love spell with a reticent partner, is not something that anyone appreciates or needs. If you cannot tell someone what your true intentions toward them actually are, you have no business working magick that involves them and you need to reexamine your path.

The law of contact also permits that whatever is done to a crystal will also have an effect on the last person to touch the crystal. This means that, with permission, you are able to work magick such as healing on a person by having them touch or hold a crystal with intention and then return it to you, first wrapping it or placing it in a pouch so that you are not directly handling it and thereby diluting or changing their energetic imprint. Then whatever action you take upon that crystal is the same thing as taking action on the person themself. It is easy to see how any witch could use this for good purposes or for bad, and you are encouraged to choose wisely between the two. Contagious magick is not an override of the free will of another person. A crystal will amplify and transfer energy, but crystal magick is not alchemy: It doesn't transmute one thing into an entirely different thing, and it doesn't create a bond out of a void.

SYMPATHETIC MAGICK AND THE LAW OF SIMILARITY

Sympathetic magick is grounded in the philosophy that "like produces like." Sympathetic magick is under the domain of the law of similarity, which is the basis of both homeopathy and the many forms of imitative magick. Witches frequently use imitative magick in spells to assist in achieving their goals and desires. Carved candles, poppets, and charm bags are some examples of imitative magick. Crystals are also used in imitative magick, particularly when they are carved to represent a specific entity or are chosen because of an auspicious color. You will see crystals carved as animals, shapes such as hearts or crescents, and effigies such as angels or deities. Crystals will also be carved with a word representing a specific goal or desired outcome. The law of similarity permits that any effect can be produced by imitating or otherwise enacting the desired effect. Modern tenets such as "dress for the job you want, not the job you have" and "fake it 'til you make it" are actually good examples of the law of similarity at work. For instance, if the currency of your country is green, using green crystals such as aventurine, prasiolite, or malachite is a way to start crafting a money drawing spell. If you are seeking a fresh start, carrying a mix of rose quartz, citrine, and heliodor or other colors of the morning sky can align you with the promise that a new day or dawn can bring. Sympathetic magick is strongly linked to color theory, and color is one of the most important visual elements that you encounter when working with crystals.

CRYSTAL COLOR THEORY

Color theory teaches that certain colors have specific, measurable, and consistent effects on the mind, psyche, and biological body. These effects have been documented widely and have remained stable over time. There is a reason that stop signs are red. Red is a color that commands attention. It is highly attractive, meaning your eye is drawn to it, and it can also be a portent. Nature will often use red as a warning. The berries of holly, yew, and some varieties of mistletoe such as *Viscum cruciatum* are all red, and they all happen to be poisonous. Blue is associated with calmness and loyalty, even longing and sorrow. Since many types of crystal occur in a multitude of colors (quartz, fluorite, and tourmaline, to name just a few), it is important to know the effects of color so that you can choose not only the right mineral type but also the correct hue for your crystal magick.

When evaluating color in crystals, you are basically attuning to two distinct characteristics: hue and saturation. Hue is the range of spectral colors that the crystal is presenting. Many crystals will exhibit a range of color and will need to be described with modifiers such as "bluish green" or "yellowish orange." By identifying the hue, you can choose crystals that are most closely aligned with your purpose. Saturation is the degree or intensity at which the hue presents itself. A pale stone will have a lower color saturation than a vividly hued stone. Saturation is also judged on a wide spectrum, and extremes in saturation or colors that are particularly vivid and intense but might be rarely seen in nature could indicate that a crystal has been dyed to achieve its color. This doesn't mean that the crystal won't work. Plenty of people manipulate color, but you should always know what you are working with. Color is not seen with our eyes. It is the brain that sees. Even people who are color-blind and cannot perceive color in the usual sense can still benefit by understanding color theory. This is because color is also a vibrational energy. We understand it through wavelength and frequency. The spectrum that we see is only what the mind can perceive through the lens of the eye. We do not and cannot perceive the entire spectrum of color wavelengths, but we can be aware of their presence and use them in magick just the same.

Color is also a kind of medicine. It is frequently used in healing because color affects people in more ways than just psychological. Color is highly evocative. It can soothe or inflame. Color is the sensual manifestation of light, and crystals are able to bend, reflect, and refract that light. Color also has spiritual connotations and has been used as a part of alchemy. Here are common color associations you can use when working with crystals:

- **Red crystals:** The color red is a color of great power. Red is used for protection, passion, survival, healing wounds, sex magick, and more. Because of its resemblance to the color of blood, red has a very dynamic and dominant energy and correlates to the life force. Agate, carnelian, beryl, ruby, tourmaline, wulfenite, and garnet can all present in various saturations of red. Red is associated with the planet Mars.
- **Orange crystals:** Orange is full of optimism and enthusiasm. Bright and cheery, it is also reminiscent of fire, which is associated with inspiration, the hearth, transformation, and warmth. Orange crystals have a signature sensuousness to them and are useful as revealers. Orange crystals include citrine, sunstone, spessartine garnet, calcite, jasper, amber, and agate. All of these and more occur in various saturations of orange. Orange is associated with Jupiter and contains strong masculine energy.
- **Yellow crystals:** Perhaps no other color of crystal radiates vitality, prosperity, and happiness quite like the color yellow. Yellow crystals

are empowering. They have uplifting energy and have an invigorating effect. Lively and warm, yellow crystals induce positive feelings. Jade, agate, jasper, calcite, topaz, sapphire, and tourmaline all occur in various saturations of yellow. Pyrite, although metallic, can also be described as having a yellow body color. Golden feldspar, golden beryl, and pale or lightly saturated citrine (sometimes called lemon quartz) are more specimens of crystals that exhibit yellow. Yellow is associated with the sun and has strong connections to joy, family, and health.

- **Green crystals:** Green is the color of growth, fertility, strength, vitality, and abundance. Gazing at a green crystal before a creative task can even result in an increase in creativity. Green is life-giving, signifies increase, and also stimulates new endeavors. Green crystals can be used in spells having to do with matters of the heart, love, healing, and attracting prosperity. Green crystals include aventurine, prasiolite, malachite, bloodstone, peridot, and emerald, to name a few.
- **Indigo crystals:** Indigo is a color associated with elevated consciousness and spiritual evolution. People who possess heightened abilities to sense and even experience the emotions of others and have psychic abilities are sometimes referred to as "indigos" or "empaths," referring to a New Age belief that people being born as the Age of Aquarius dawns will have particular gifts. Dark blue and indigo crystals are useful for opening and attuning the third eye, the center of psychic and sacred sight. Sodalite, azurite, lapis lazuli, and iolite are examples of indigo crystals.
- **Purple crystals:** Purple is associated with royalty, and, as such, purple crystals have a certain elevated energy. Purple is both calming and invigorating, which makes purple crystals extremely useful in meditation: those moments when you need to be relaxed but not tired, calm but energized. Purple crystals are excellent for ritual and high magick as they can help you tap into the higher powers. Sugilite, charoite, fluorite, and amethyst are examples of purple crystals.
- **White crystals:** If you are interested in attuning with your higher self and exploring spiritual consciousness, white crystals are a great place to start. White crystals represent potential because white is the color that contains all other colors. Selenite, apophyllite, some varieties of moonstone, agate, jasper, and onyx are examples of white crystals.

- **Brown crystals:** Brown crystals are frequently used for grounding and protection magick, particularly protection of the home. Carrying a brown crystal while traveling can direct energy into an eventual safe passage home. Smoky quartz, tiger's eye, unakite, and some varieties of topaz, garnet, agate, and jasper are examples of brown crystals.
- **Clear crystals:** Clear crystals are wonderful tools that you can project your desires onto. They are useful in manifestation magick, in honing your intuition and insight, and for spells or situations where clarity is needed. Clear crystals can help dispel confusion, improve focus, and assist with goal setting. Clear quartz is the most common clear crystal.
- **Black crystals:** Black crystals have many uses. Their opacity and sheen make them highly suitable for scrying. They are used in shadow work, protection magick, reversing spells, and defensive spells, as well as for grounding energy and dispelling negativity. Black is a powerful color that has associations with mystery, the night sky, and all manner of things wondrous and nocturnal. And although black is technically defined as the absence of color, this very trait invites the bearer of the black crystal to engage in deep introspection, to consider the lack of attachment that can truly free the spirit. Black also represents death and mourning, making black crystals a potential source of comfort for those who are grieving. Black crystals include onyx, obsidian, and jet.

CRYSTAL PLANETARY CORRESPONDENCES

This section will provide you with some of the attributes and associations among crystals, their planetary correspondences, and their application in creating a personal crystal charm. This will help you access and adapt information for crafting your own unique practice of crystal magick. For example, if you want to dedicate some of the crystals you already have for magickal workings, it is helpful to know what attributes they already possess and what conditions of mind, body, or spirit they are anecdotally useful for. In later chapters, you will learn different types of spells and charms that incorporate crystals. If you want to enact any of these spells but lack the exact type of mineral that is recommended, use this section to find appropriate substitutions. Remember that it is not necessary to run out and spend a large amount of money on crystals in order to use them for magick. Some people really enjoy collecting crystals just for the sake of collecting them and never plan to use them at all, while others use crystals only as magickal and ritual tools. And because crystals are so ancient and so powerful, it is perfectly fine to clear and charge one crystal over and over again for different reasons. The only time you may want to part with a crystal is if you want to give it to someone else as a gift, or if you have used it for severing some kind of connection and need to remove it from your space in order to complete a spell.

Planetary Correspondences

If you enjoy reading your horoscope, or if you cast your own charts, you will benefit from learning which planets have correspondences with certain crystals. Metallic asteroids are known to contain iron, which is the element that gives many crystals unique colors. So connected are the planets and crystals that vendors sell polished crystal spheres in sets to resemble the solar system. Some common correlations between the planets and crystals are:

CRYSTALS ASSOCIATED WITH PLANETS

- Mercury: beryl, opal
- Venus: peridot, emerald
- Earth: agate, jasper
- Mars: garnet, bloodstone
- Jupiter: amethyst, lapis lazuli
- Saturn: onyx, jet
- Uranus: iolite, kyanite
- Neptune: sodalite, sapphire
- Pluto: obsidian, hematite

In ancient Egypt, after oracles began to lose their widespread appeal and as the popularity of astrology began to rise, planetary correspondences with crystals and minerals were recorded. From a papyrus dated to the second or third century, scholar James Evans, who is a historian of astronomy at the University of Puget Sound in Tacoma, Washington, has provided a detailed interpretation of an excerpt that explains how crystals and minerals were used to represent specific planets when casting horoscopes on an astrology board.

Specifically, the following correspondences were noted:

- Sun: gold
- Moon: silver
- Mercury: turquoise
- Venus: lapis lazuli
- Mars: red onyx
- Jupiter: quartz
- Saturn: obsidian

The fact that these correspondence charts are different does not mean that one of them is right and that one of them is wrong. It means that astrologers and magick workers determined correlations based on their knowledge, what they were able to access, and the needs of the time. Their understanding of the world and the crystals they were familiar with all factored into how they incorporated crystals and magick. What worked for ancient Egyptians was different from what worked for people in the Middle Ages, which was different from what worked in the Renaissance, and those are all different from what we know and need today. Modern witches have every right to determine the correspondences that work for them. If a crystal speaks to you and carries a specific energetic charge, be it emotional or spiritual or supernatural, do not confuse information with your intuition by valuing one over the other. After all, who do you think made correspondences to begin with? People with occult knowledge and abilities in magick with a talent for crystals and planets and for predicting and affecting outcomes.

Personal Crystal Planetary Charm

To create one type of crystal charm that you can use for your own personal expression, figure out the ruling planet of your zodiac sign and choose a crystal from either the modern or ancient planetary correspondence chart. Then, using the zodiac and birthstone charts, add one crystal for your zodiac sign and one for your birth month. You can find several appropriate crystal choices in the tables in Chapter 10. For example, for a person born in January under the sign of Aquarius, the choice of crystals might look like this:

- Garnet
- Amethyst
- Onyx
- Kyanite

Once you have decided which crystals you will work with for your own personal crystal profile, you can keep the stones on your altar or sacred space or carry them with you in a charm bag. You can also take this exercise further and use the crystals for any number of purposes—for instance, to inspire you, to remind you of who you are, or as an aid with decision-making, or to assist you on your path of self-discovery, initiation, or general awakening to esoteric and occult ideas.

Give each crystal a name, one that resonates with an aspect of yourself, your endeavors, or just things that bring you pleasure and make you happy. Then, in moments of doubt or confusion, reach for a crystal at random and see what it is telling you.

Chapter 3

CREATING YOUR CRYSTAL COLLECTION

Now that you have learned about the origins of the different kinds of magickal practices that are necessary for successful modern crystal magick, building your own crystal collection is the next step. Whether you are proficient in working magick with crystals or you are just starting out, there is always more to learn and new discoveries and associations to integrate.

Crystals can be manipulated and cut to maximize their effectiveness in occult and esoteric work. Crystal formations in their natural state hold a distinct and powerful energy; however, when a crystal is cut and polished, it takes on a far more refined energy and can be dedicated for a very specific purpose. In this chapter, you will gain valuable information on the many different types of crystals that you are likely to encounter, such as tumbled stones, crystal points, spheres, towers or pillars, geodes, and slices. And as you build your collection, whether large or small, you will gain knowledge on what characteristics to consider (such as heat treatment, cuts, and if a crystal is natural) as well as on arrangements and displays to maximize your enjoyment of your collection so that you can use it to your fullest potential.

CHOOSING YOUR CRYSTALS

Starting a crystal collection is an exercise in self-awareness and personal preference. There is no criterion more important than what you find pleasing. Preference can be purely visual or entirely intuitive. You can select the crystals that you desire to work with by considering their shape, size, color, or energy. You do not really need to base your decisions on anything other than your own feelings or the general sense of what you would like to accomplish.

You might begin your collection by looking for contrasting shapes or colors. You might also want to study Part 2 and get a stronger sense of the emotional and spiritual associations of dozens of crystals. You might even have a particular spell or specific magickal working in mind and you are seeking a certain type of crystal that will aid the sacred work. And in reality, your crystal collection might begin with a little bit of all of the above: You might want aesthetic crystals, working crystals, crystals as sacred tools, and crystals for adornment.

CRYSTAL SHAPES

When most people think of crystals, typically the six-sided prism with the pyramid top comes to mind. In reality, crystals and the magickal tools made with and from them occur in many configurations that are either pieces of or alterations of the natural formations. Just because a crystal has been altered does not mean that it is not useful. While some of these shapes are naturally occurring, many will bear the mark of the human hand and are no less a testament to the power of transformation. (After all, altering stones for certain purposes has been a practice since crystals were discovered.) While natural crystals are certainly desirable, you will find that there are different applications for different cuts and that each unique shape carries a certain kind of magick all its own.

If you plan to collect crystals, you will undoubtedly be drawn to different sizes and shapes. The many varieties, whether they are in their natural rough form or cut and polished, all have different applications. For example, crystal chips and tumbled stones are small and lend themselves readily to charm bags. A crystal sphere can be a talisman if it is small and a divination tool if it is large. A pillar makes an impressive altarpiece or a powerful focal point for meditation. To work crystal magick, you will find that you need different sizes and shapes for different magickal spells and that some crystal shapes lend themselves to your individual craft more readily than others.

Chips

Crystal chips are small fragments of a mineral that have sheared off along a cleavage plane (where crystal faces in the lattice meet). They retain all the characteristics and color of their intact counterparts. Affordable and plentiful, crystal chips are extremely versatile and very useful in witchcraft. They can be included in potions such as oil blends used in magick spells. They can be used in candle magick by adding them to molten wax or on top of a freshly poured candle by pressing them into the wax after it has cooled but before it has completely hardened. And they can be used in jar spells, in charm bags, and in altar craft.

Drusy

Drusy (also spelled "druzy") describes tiny crystal clusters that grow on a matrix or host mineral. These crystal clusters are extremely small and numerous, creating a sparkling appearance of a stone that is coated with hundreds of crystal points. Although drusy crystals are very small, they still have a strong resemblance to their larger crystal cluster counterparts. Found inside of geodes, drusy are frequently used in talismans and jewelry. In magick, drusy can represent community, extended families, and networks of covens because all of the tiny points of light are joined together.

Tumbled Stones

Tumbled stones are crystals that have been exposed to moving water for an extended period of time. Tumbled stones are generally plentiful and not particularly expensive. They are typically made from crystals that might have endured some damage during the mining process or perhaps do not have the color saturation or transparency to make them rare. Tumbled stones are always very glossy and smooth and rarely have their crystal faces, as they have been worn away by the energy of the water and rubbed smooth through contact with other stones. Crystals can be tumbled naturally by a river, but it is far more common for crystals to be tumbled by machinery: A quantity of rough crystals is placed inside a watertight cylinder filled with another material such as pumice or steel shot (small smooth pieces of metal resembling ball bearings), and the cylinder is placed on a belt-and-wheel system that keeps it in perpetual motion until the polishing cycle is complete. Rock tumblers are not prohibitively expensive; they vary greatly in size and effectiveness. The larger the tumbler, the more crystals it can accommodate. Many hobbyists enjoy finding and tumbling their own crystals. Since tumbled crystals are typically small, they are excellent for use in charm bags, jar spells, and parts of matrices, and can even be used as talismans or in jewelry.

Palm Stones

Usually slightly larger than tumbled stones, palm stones have a defined oval shape and are sometimes flat or slightly concave with a small divot to encourage stroking. Interestingly enough, the word "divot" comes from Sanskrit, meaning "reaching for heaven." Sometimes called "worry stones," palm stones are a tool of mindfulness. Palm stones are most frequently carried by the witch in hand or kept in a pocket. Palm stones, made from a variety of minerals, are used to self-soothe and focus. In Japan, it is customary to have a "feeling stone," which is carried in the pocket in order to bring about a sense of calmness, comfort, and peace.

Geodes

Geodes are hollow pockets that surround small drusy clusters. These empty chambers of metamorphic rock can reveal wondrous crystals kept within. Left unbroken, a geode can be quite unremarkable, appearing as an ordinary round rock. When broken open, a geode will reveal a coating of small crystal clusters. Geodes are often cut in half to reveal their inner beauty and mystery. While collecting and breaking open geodes is a cherished hobby among rock hounds, for witches, the geode can represent a cycle of completion or attainment. Useful in house blessing or hearth magick, a geode calls us to contemplate safety and fulfillment, as its contents are protected, then revealed. A geode is a physical manifestation of an ideal environment for growth.

Slices

Crystal slices are cross sections of larger crystals and appear as flat crystals with a uniform depth. They are frequently dyed bright colors and are sometimes incorporated into objects such as table top decor, jewelry, and windchimes. Slices can be used magickally as charging plates, as a place to set offerings on your altar, and even as scrying mirrors if they are dark enough.

Crystal Points

A crystal point is a crystal that has grown large enough to be impressive on its own, independent of its cluster formation. Crystal points are usually the natural formation of a six-sided crystal with a pyramidal termination point, but sometimes the natural facets are polished so that the facet edges are very sharp and well-defined. You may often encounter crystals that are cut to resemble natural points. Natural crystal points come in a variety of sizes, from very small to very large. The larger the point, the more expensive it will be. When choosing crystal points, you will notice there is some irregularity in the faces of the crystal. This is usually an indication that the crystal is natural. If you see a crystal point that is too regular or too perfect, it is probably not a point but a less valuable chunk of mineral cut to look like a point. Crystal points are frequently used in pendulums for divination. They are also used in the tips of wands for directing energy. Crystal points are conducive to communication with spirits and oracles, and a variety of other types of spells.

DOUBLE-TERMINATED CRYSTAL POINTS

Double-terminated crystals follow the six-sided pyramidal formation but have points on both ends, known as dipyramidal termination. Herkimer diamonds (a misnomer because Herkimer diamonds are not diamonds at all) are a good example. Commonly found in upstate New York, Herkimer diamonds are named for their geographic origin (Herkimer County) and their appearance: unusually clear, and always double terminated, which means it will have two distinct points at opposite ends. Apatite is another example of a dipyramidal crystal. Double-terminated crystals are ideal for channeling and divination: Their natural formation is a two-way street with both ends culminating in a perfect pyramid point. Double-terminated crystals represent the "as it is above, so is it below" principle of witchcraft and are excellent for use in pendulums and in psychometry. Double-terminated crystals are usually small to medium in size.

Harmonizers

Harmonizers are crystals cut and polished into a cylindrical shape. Harmonizers can be cut from a wide array of crystals and are often used in pairs. Harmonizers range in size with the diameter of the base of the cylinder usually measuring 1–2 inches and the length about 4–6 inches. Used to create a state of balance, harmonizers are used during meditation with one held in each hand, bringing about a euphoric layered experience, as their name suggests. Harmonizer crystal pairs are chosen for their desired metaphysical effects.

Healers

Healers are similar to harmonizers in size but differ in shape. Healers are elongated tapers with a slightly conical shape but rounded on each end. Healers are used in meditation and also massage. They are polished smooth, and the rounded ends are used to stimulate pressure points on the body. Healers are also used horizontally by rolling with gentle pressure across muscles and skin tissue. Golden feldspar is a popular crystal often seen cut in this shape. Referred to as "golden healers," these crystals promote self-care, happiness, and balance.

Spheres

Depending on the size, spheres can be very expensive. This is because they are cut from the "heart" of the crystal, meaning that the rough mineral has to be large enough to have a sphere cut out of it. And the larger the crystal, the rarer it will be and therefore the more expensive. Also, cutting and polishing a large crystal into a sphere takes skill, so a crystal sphere is going to be more expensive than a crystal point of a similar size. Crystal spheres are used for gazing and scrying, for seeing beyond the veil, and for meditation and divination.

Towers or Pillars

Towers, also called pillars, resemble very large points, except that they are polished flat on the bottom and can stand on their own, making them very desirable altar pieces. Towers are used in manifestation magick and in directing energy. They can also be used as "markers" to honor deity or spiritual energy. Often shaped like an obelisk, pillars can be cut from a variety of minerals and therefore will show a large range in price. Crystal pillars and towers are symbols of power. "Towers" and "pillars" are used interchangeably, as they are describing only the cut and size.

Carved Crystals

You may find in your searching for the right crystals that a lot of crystals are carved to resemble specific things. Crystals carved to resemble hearts, animals, scarabs, mythological creatures, skulls, flowers, and the like can all be used in imitative magick. Using a crystal carved into a specific shape gives a very literal meaning to its natural attributes. Carved crystals provide an entry point into crystal magick in that they already resemble a specific form, and as a witch, you can relate to them through the form that they are taking on. In addition to the shape, you also need to consider the type of crystal that is used. For instance, a crystal carved into a heart can represent love or vitality, and the type of crystal that the heart is carved from will add another, deeper layer to its metaphysical associations.

Treated Crystals

You will find that many natural crystals are altered to improve their appearance. For example, rose quartz tends to occur naturally in pale pink, short, stubby clusters. Natural rose quartz usually has a lot of internal inclusions, making clear specimens very rare. If you encounter a bright pink crystal pillar that is described as rose quartz, it has most likely been cut and dyed, meaning that the shape was cut out of a rough stone and made to look like a tall crystal point and the color has been enhanced. Similarly, a lot of amethyst is heat treated after it comes out of the ground. Heat can intensify the purple colors of amethyst. While these treatments are common, they are definitely worth asking about, especially if you are thinking about acquiring a crystal and the color seems too intense to be natural. Ethical people will tell you if a crystal has been heat treated or dyed.

You should also be on the lookout for products that are called crystals but aren't. For example, leaded crystal is a type of glass that is made from molten quartz combined with lead oxide. The lead increases the quartz's ability to break light into its spectral colors. Leaded crystal does contain quartz and retains some characteristics of natural quartz, but it is very heavily processed. The quartz used in leaded crystal starts out as sand and can be anywhere from 25–40 percent lead. Opalite is another example of a man-made stone that has a strong resemblance to crystal. Often sold as a crystal alongside natural stones, opalite is a type of synthetic glass that has a strong visual resemblance to crystals such as moonstone, opal, and quartz.

HOW CRYSTALS CHOOSE YOU

Sometimes you may find yourself drawn to a certain crystal without even knowing why. In addition to having a physical body, you also have a field of energy that emanates from you and surrounds you. Some people interpret this energy as aura. An aura can be felt through intuition, and some people can even see it. Auras have also been captured by photography, and the lens, whether it is the human eye or a camera lens, will frequently interpret the aura as a color. The aura is rarely monochromatic; most often it appears as spectral with varying degrees of saturation. The aura can be an amalgam of several colors with one dominant hue presenting prominently, and the color of the aura can change depending on your state of mind, emotions, or environment. When your energetic field resonates at the same vibrational level as a crystal, it's possible to feel an immediate harmony, an attraction that is immediate and feels right. This is one way that crystals may choose you!

Crystal Magnification

"Like attracts like," and a crystal can receive and match your energy signature and even add to it to make both sources of energetic vibration or aura (yours and the crystal's) a little stronger.

Another way a crystal may choose you is if there is an energetic deficiency or some sense of lack that needs to be balanced or fulfilled. A crystal's vibrational energy may seek the place where it ought to be, similar to the way that water will seek its own level. If there is some kind of need or scarcity you are projecting, and the energy vibration you lack is the same as or similar to the energy signature the crystal is emanating, the crystal then may seek to redress that feeling of lack and put itself into that space in order to create balance. The quest for balance is inherent in nature, and crystals are natural objects. You are part of the natural world, but you are often pulled astray from your state of balance by the material world.

You can unintentionally create undesirable situations and environments due to the intrusion of the material plane. Think of any time you have entered a ritual or a library or any kind of temple or place of worship. Your energy immediately begins to attune to your surroundings. And if you come in with chaotic energy, there is always a guide to direct your energy vibration toward the harmonic level. The priestess witch will cut you in. The librarian will tell you to hush. When you're working with crystals, the temple is your mind, body, and spirit. The crystal is the librarian. The crystal vibration will seek the energy that is out of alignment in order to set it right.

Sometimes a crystal will choose you through fate. These are the stones you will find unexpectedly. They will come to you as gifts or chance encounters, they'll appear in your path through luck, or they'll find other ways to you. To receive a crystal is always auspicious. It is coming into your hands either because it is already resonating with you or because it is part of your path to balance and fulfillment.

Crystals can also assist you through difficulty. They may choose you when you are facing some kind of hardship or breakdown by coming into your possession at a crucial time. The way crystals bend light is a comforting reminder that change is always within reach. Until you begin to work with a crystal in a spell, it will always have a default neutral energy.

HOW TO FIND CRYSTALS FOR SPECIFIC NEEDS

Locating the perfect crystal, or at least the appropriate crystal, is going to be indelibly linked to your specific intention. Whether you want crystals for ambience or because they make you feel invigorated or calm, or because you want to use them in magick, ritual, and spells, the clearer you are in your intention, the greater your success in locating the right crystal will be. Make room for the unexpected. You may go in search of one crystal and discover that you can't find exactly what you are looking for. Remember that crystals are natural gifts from the earth and unless you are looking for something carved, cut, or calibrated to a specific size and shape, you will need to appreciate the unique qualities and energies that individual crystals possess.

CLEANSING, CLEARING, AND CHARGING YOUR CRYSTALS

Once you find the crystal that you want to work with, you will want to make it your own by ritual means, not just by purchasing it. Whether you are seeking an aventurine to enhance creative inspiration, a rose quartz heart for openness to love, or an amethyst sphere for gazing into, there are steps you will want to take in order to dedicate your discoveries to magick.

Since many crystals are highly conductive, there is a good chance that whatever crystal you come across and plan to add to your collection has already had quite a lot of energy running through it. Some of these residual energy signatures might be discovery, destruction, transport, or any other number of occurrences that may have left energetic traces still resonating through the lattice. While any of these lingering energies may or may not prove useful in magick, the point is that you just don't know how the crystal has been handled and by whom or by how many and what intentions it might already be charged with. Therefore, it is prudent to assume that any crystal you plan to use in personal magick will need to be cleared or cleansed before you can charge it with intentional energy. Cleansing and clearing always come before charging, and it is important to know how to do all three.

Cleansing

Crystals come out of the earth and when they do, they are often covered in debris and dirt; therefore, cleaning your crystals is a necessary first step. A crystal chosen from a shop on a shelf is bound to have accumulated dust, which will dull its appearance. It will also have oil from the fingertips of those who previously touched it. Crystals that don't show any obvious outside dust or film still need to be cleaned. Think of your crystal as you would any other personal, valuable, or sacred item. You wouldn't buy a crystal wine glass and use it before you washed it. You would wash any utensil or personal care item (especially a magickal one) that you brought into your house before using it, and crystals are no different. In fact, you could say that cleaning your crystals is equally important if you plan to do more than just collect. Since you are bringing crystals into your home as magickal tools, they deserve even more care and attention. You would wash anything that you intended to come into contact with your body, and crystals will come into contact with your etheric body, your aura, your spiritual essence, so clean them.

Cleaning your crystals is an important first step. If you are washing them in your sink, put a washcloth over the drain and gently put the crystals on top of the washcloth. Let the water run over them as you handle them, and use a little bit of natural soap or detergent, nothing too harsh. As the water runs down the drain, allow this to turn into an esoteric exercise. Envision all residual surface energy leaving with the running water. Have another cloth handy to place your crystals on to dry. Try to avoid touching them until you decide on the method you would like to use for clearing.

CRYSTAL CLEANING DOS AND DON'TS

- Do use warm or tepid water and a soft cloth or toothbrush.
- Don't use anything abrasive.
- Do use running water.
- Don't wash your crystals over an open drain. Place a washcloth over the drain opening.
- Do use a small amount of natural soap.
- Don't use any harsh chemicals.
- Do use a soft cloth to dry your crystals.
- Do use a natural degreaser such as a cotton swab moistened with white vinegar to remove sticky residue from crystals that may have had adhesive labels stuck on them by the seller.

Clearing

Clearing is different from cleaning. Cleaning is removing physical dirt or dust. Clearing is removing the residual lingering energy imprinted on the crystal by anyone who has previously touched it, transported it, used it, or sold it. Clearing is very important because it will not only give your crystal a type of reset, but it will also start the process of developing your personal connection to the crystal. Since the law of contact permits that a crystal will still contain energy even without proximity, clearing is an essential step before using your crystals for magick. There are many ways to clear a crystal. Four of the most common are through smoke, water, earth, and sound. The method you choose will be highly dependent on where and how you live. For stubborn residual energy, you may find that you need to use more than one clearing technique. If you clear the crystal, but your intuition tells you that it is not ready for a new magickal application, you can continue with another clearing technique. This is more common with crystals that have been handled by many different people. Of the four main clearing techniques described here, smoke and sound clearing are the most accessible, while earth and water require certain conditions. Depending on the number, size, and intended use, it is generally best to clear crystals one at a time unless they are small. For example, a bag of crystal chips could be cleared as a single entity as long as they were all kept together.

SMOKE CLEARING

Smoke clearing is easy to perform and effective; however, care should be taken when burning anything. Stick incense or bundled herbs can be used for smoke clearing, but when used as part of a magick ritual (and you can consider smoke clearing to be the first type of magick that you will enact with your crystal), respect and attention must be given. For example, there is considerable controversy around the use of white sage. White sage is the go-to for smoke clearing for a lot of people due to its effectiveness; however, many people believe it is disrespectful to Indigenous cultures to appropriate their rituals and magick if you are not a participating member of their culture. Also, white sage has been connected to overharvesting. If you are not from an Indigenous culture, it is preferable to use something else. Palo santo is another popular and well-known ingredient in smoke clearing, but since it grows throughout Central and South America, it is associated with shamanism, brujería, and Latin American Catholicism. While palo santo is not endangered, it is considered sacred, and using sacred ritual ingredients from a specific culture is a point of contention for many people. The modern practice of witchcraft is extremely syncretic by nature, as it is often practiced as an amalgamation of modified rituals from ancient and modern cultures. In the case of smoke clearing, move according to your conscience with knowledge and empathy and use herbs wisely.

There are two basic ways to perform a smoke clearing on crystals:

1. Using powdered incense, charcoal, and a heat-safe container, light the charcoal with a match or lighter and let it smolder until it glows red. Blow on it gently to create a link between your breath and the

combustion of the coal. Sprinkle a pinch of incense on the charcoal. Do this very sparingly, as loose incense on charcoal can emit a great amount of smoke very quickly. As the smoke wafts in the air, hold your crystal 6 inches or more above the coal and let the smoke float over the surfaces of the crystal as you turn it over and over so that all sides are exposed to the smoke.

2. Light a candle. Using stick incense or bundled herbs, light the end of the bundle from the candle, allow it to burn just a little bit, and then blow it out gently. Continue to blow if necessary to keep the herbs or incense glowing and smoldering. Hold the bundle of herbs or incense in one hand and your crystal in the other using your fingers. Holding the crystal delicately with your fingertips will give more of its surface access to the clearing ability of the smoke. Rotate the hand holding the bundle clockwise around the hand holding the crystal. Light the bundle repeatedly from the candle if necessary (not all herbs will smolder for a long enough time to do a thorough clearing). After you make a few passes around your crystal-holding hand with the smoke, rotate both hands around one another in a "rolling" motion to finish the clearing.

After smoke clearing your crystal, it should be free of residual energy and ready to use for your own purpose, or you might intuit that it needs additional exposure to elements. You can use the elements of water and earth to clear a crystal as well.

WATER CLEARING

Water is the cradle of life and has very strong associations with magick. In witchcraft, in order to break a magick spell or a curse, it is customary to pass through a stand of water. This is not meant to imply that your crystals are cursed, just to emphasize the power and effectiveness of water for removing unwanted energy. Christians use water as the primary element in the baptism ritual of forgiveness for any and all transgressions, further adding to the power of the law of contact and affirming that contact between water and an object has positive magickal benefits. Holy water is used in a similar way. Water is the conduit of blessing. If water has been blessed, then anyone who anoints themself with the blessed water is also receiving the blessing by coming into contact with the water. For clearing a crystal, you can use running water, standing water, charged water, or any combination of the three.

RUNNING WATER

Running water can be from a river, a faucet, an ocean, or any other body of water with a current. The most important aspect is that the water is moving, so that it can carry away the residual energy that the crystal may contain. If you are clearing your crystal or crystals in a natural body of water, you can use one of these techniques:

- Hold the crystal loosely by securely cupping your hands around it and enter the water with your crystal, allowing for total immersion in the flow. Keep tension in your fingers and allow them to spread ever so slightly so the water moves freely around your crystal.
- If for whatever reason you can't physically go in the water, secure your crystals in a muslin pouch. Run a string through the drawstring loops of the pouch if you need additional length and allow your crystals to enter the flow while holding the string securely so that they do not get swept away.
- After clearing your crystals with water, either keep them in their pouch and allow them to dry naturally or wrap them in a soft cloth and avoid touching them until you are ready to use them in magick, provided that this is your intention. If the crystals are meant to serve an aesthetic purpose, you can place them where you wish.

COLLECTED WATER

It is possible to use water without a current, but you will need to either take action to create movement so the clearing can take place or rely on evaporation, which takes longer. Standing water such as gathered rainwater or snowfall is ideal, but you can also use spring water, purified water, or tap water. Avoid stagnant water such as in ponds or puddles. Stagnant energy is not what you want, and while stagnant water does host life and change, it's usually in the form of mosquitoes and bacteria. Here are the steps for clearing with collected water.

Clearing with Collected Water

You Will Need

- Crystal
- 2 vessels that can be interchangeably used for pouring and receiving
- Water for magickal intent; some suggestions are leaving out a large jar during a rainfall and capturing some rainwater, getting a good scoop of snow from the first or last snowfall of the season, or using bottled spring water

Directions

1. Hold your crystal over the receiving (empty) vessel. This can be your chalice from your altar or a cup or a bowl. With the crystal between your fingertips, pour water from the other vessel over your crystal, catching it in the receiving vessel.
2. Repeat the process, pouring the water over again until your crystal is cleared. You may speak your intention as you pour, such as:

Waters of renewal
Waters of transformation
Waters of rebirth
Clear and cleanse
Heal and mend.
What has come before is now released.
What has occurred before has been forever changed.
Dedicated anew in this moment
By my hand,
For my purpose
And mine alone.

CHARGED WATER

It is possible to imbue crystals with mystical, celestial, and lunar energy by using water according to the law of contact. This method takes a long time and will appeal to the more patient practitioner who is in no hurry to use their crystal right away. The benefit of using charged water and evaporation clearing is in its celestial and transformational energy.

Leaving a bowl of water outside under the full moon overnight is one way to charge water with lunar energy. You can also charge water in the sun by letting it come into contact with sunshine during the height of the sun's intensity, typically between 10:00 a.m. and 2:00 p.m. The moon is often associated with feminine energy and the sun with masculine energy. Choosing a method of charging water with intention adds another dimension of magick to your interaction with your crystals and establishes them as magickal tools even before you start working with them in earnest. To clear a crystal with charged water, follow these directions.

Clearing with Charged Water

You Will Need

- Crystal(s)
- Vessel (bowl, jar, or chalice) that can hold your crystals
- Water (enough to cover the crystals)
- For solar water, a bright and sunny day
- For moon water, an almanac, a moon phase app, or direct observation that allows you to ascertain the phase of the moon
- Windowsill or a safe, level, and stable place where the vessel can be left outside

Directions

1. Place the crystal or crystals in the holding vessel and cover them with water.
2. Place the holding vessel outside under the sunlight or moonlight.
3. Take the vessel to your altar or sacred meditation space after it has been exposed to the light of the celestial body of your choice.
4. Allow the water to evaporate over a period of several days or several weeks.
5. Remove your crystals from the vessel once the water is gone.

Feel free to combine elements from several crystal clearing techniques. You should choose the one that resonates with you, is feasible, and is compatible with your practice. You can also modify these steps. For example, you might want to use charged water, but you don't want to wait for evaporation. In that case, use the charged water but incorporate the directions for standing water. Use movement to add the kinetic energy necessary for a good clearing. Also, if your standing water is scarce and you don't have a jar full of rainwater, add a few drops from your collected water to bottled water or faucet water in order to raise its vibration. The two most important things are your action and your intention and not the nature and amount of water you are using.

EARTH CLEARING

Deep earth is the birthplace of crystals, and sending them back to their source for a reset is an effective clearing method. Placing a crystal in contact with the living earth is a very effective way to reset its energy signature. Earth contact provides transformations, grounding, healing, and energizing. It is also very easy to perform.

Earth Clearing

You Will Need

- Access to land, or a deep flower pot if private property is not accessible to you
- Garden trowel
- Crystal
- Marker or indicator such as a garden stake or a distinct stick

Directions

1. Choose an auspicious phase of the moon to start your clearing. The moon phase should align with your intended use of the crystal. For example, if you are working on new beginnings or releasing things that no longer serve you, start on the new moon. If you are going to start a series of manifestations and calling situations or events into being, begin on a full moon.
2. Dig a hole in the earth with the trowel and bury the crystal at a depth that covers the crystal completely and will not be easily uncovered by wind, rain, or animals.
3. Mark the spot with your indicator.
4. Allow your crystal to remain undisturbed for one complete lunar cycle (twenty-eight days).
5. Retrieve your crystal when the moon phase has returned to the phase where you began your clearing.
6. Follow the directions for cleaning your crystal.

The electromagnetic field of the earth has a powerful effect on anything that it comes into contact with. It is possible to reset any crystal (and even yourself!) by allowing for prolonged direct contact with the earth. There is nothing more grounding than direct contact with the earth. To understand the efficacy of this method, try standing with your bare feet on the earth for any length of time. You will notice a change in your energy after just twenty or thirty seconds. Allowing your crystal to have a lunation cycle of contact with the earth is allowing it to be "reborn" (you are returning it to its source, in a sympathetic way) and dedicated for your personal use.

SOUND CLEARING

Using sound vibration is another way to clear your crystal. It is fast and easy but should also be done with care. There are several basic methods for clearing a crystal with sound, and few of them require special tools. Sound is simply a result of energy moving through a substance. Similar to how some eyes have the ability to convert the wavelength and frequency of light into colors that are discerned by our brains, most people are also able to convert electrical energy into mechanical energy in the form of sound wavelengths through their eardrums. People with compromised eardrums can also experience sound through purely vibrational energy without hearing it. Sound vibrations are powerful. They can be felt in the physical body and produce immediate effects. Sound can be used to calm, to quell, to inspire, to invigorate, to focus, and to create feelings of centeredness and peace. Allowing sound vibrations to permeate your crystal is an effective way to clear your crystal and is particularly useful for clearing a crystal needed for immediate use.

Here are different methods that you can use to clear your crystal with sound.

TAPPING

To clear a crystal by tapping, hold it loosely in your hand and strike it against a surface so that it makes a sound while placing your other hand over your heart. Tapping needs to be done with care because most crystals will have cleavage planes, where crystal faces in the lattice meet. It is very easy to break a crystal if you strike it on a cleavage plane. It is not necessary for the sound vibration to be loud; it just has to be regular. Once you get a feel for gentle tapping, find a rhythm that resonates with you. This can be the beat to your favorite song, a chant that you use in meditation, or even your heartbeat. Close your eyes and repeat the pattern, allowing time for you to get into a steady rhythm.

CUPPING AND CLAPPING

You can clear a crystal with sound by holding it in a cupped hand and then clapping with your other hand, also cupped. This only works with tumbled stones, spheres of 1½ inches in diameter or less, and small points that can be easily held. Clapping your hands while they are cupped produces a comforting, hollow sound at various pitches depending on how and where your hands meet. As with the tapping technique, you will probably find that a natural rhythm emerges from this exercise, like a steady heartbeat. The repetition is trance inducing and can allow you to also clear your mind. Holding the crystal establishes a link, and vibrations from the clapping travel through the crystal, bringing it into alignment with your purpose. When your mind is clear and you feel centered, you can bet that your crystal has also been cleared.

USING A TUNING FORK

Tuning forks are extremely useful in that they allow you to quantify the precise vibrational energy that you are using. While it is not imperative that you know the exact frequency that you are clearing your crystal with, there are certain frequencies that are more auspicious than others. For example, the frequency 528 hertz (Hz) is widely described as a healing tone or a "love frequency." Listening to the tone can create an immediate sense of mental calm, relaxation, and stillness. You can obtain a tuning fork that resonates at this frequency and use the vibration to clear your crystal by striking the tines and then holding the base of the tuning fork (which is the stem opposite of the tines) directly against your crystal. The great thing about using a tuning fork to clear a crystal is that you can still feel the vibration long after the sound of the vibration is no longer audible. Allow your crystal to absorb the full length of the frequency and repeat as often as you need to until you feel the effects of the energy transfer.

After you have cleared your crystal, try holding it to your heart, striking the tines of the tuning fork, and then holding the base against the crystal while you are still holding the crystal to your chest. You will feel the vibrations travel through the crystal and into your body, allowing your physical body to attune to your crystal through the healing vibration.

USING AN AUDIO SPEAKER

If you have an external audio speaker, you can place your crystal on top of the speaker and play the 528 Hz frequency. You are also free to choose whatever frequency resonates with you. You may want to choose a favorite song, a chant, a galdr (which is a rune chant), or music that inspires you. Allow the beautiful vibrations of sound to travel through your crystal, carrying with them all the residual unknown energy into the ether and away so that your crystal is renewed and ready to be dedicated to its new purpose.

Quick Clear

After you have cleaned and cleared your crystals and have used them in your magick, you may find from time to time that they need some attention and refreshing from the demands of magickal work. For example, if you are reconfiguring your altar because of the change of seasons or to enact a new or different type of spell, it is not necessary to do a rigorous clearing of your crystals, but you will want to examine them and attend to any issues such as dust from incense ashes or dullness from repeated handling. Here is a quick and easy way to refresh your crystals that you are already using for magick.

Lavender Crystal Clearing Spell

You Will Need

- 3–4 drops lavender essential oil (you may use a different oil if you have another purpose in mind, but lavender is typically used for magickal cleaning)
- Large bowl, filled about ⅔ full with warm water
- Your crystals
- Small hand towel
- Soft toothbrush

Directions

1. Add the lavender oil to the warm water. Give it a quick stir with your fingers to disperse the oil a bit.
2. Place your crystals in the bowl one at time. Pay attention to the level of the water. Generally, a large bowl such as a mixing bowl can fit three to four (2½- to 4-inch) crystals before it overflows. If you are

cleaning a crystal cluster, place it (very gently) with the matrix facing up and the crystal points facing down in the water. This will allow gravity to do some of the work in cleaning the crystal.

3. Spread the hand towel in front of the bowl.
4. Remove the crystals one by one and inspect them. For crystal clusters, you may need to use the soft toothbrush to get in the recesses between the points. If a crystal needs a gentle brushing, attend to those areas and then place the crystal back in the bowl to rinse it. You might need to agitate the crystals a little if they were dusty. Keep them in the water for a short time because you don't want any debris or dust to resettle.
5. Remove crystals from the bowl and place them upside down or on their side so that the water is more readily drawn into the hand towel.
6. Allow your crystals to air-dry and then put them back on your altar, in their display case, or in their new configuration wherever that may be.

When and How to Use Oil with Crystals

Crystals such as emeralds with inclusions that approach or touch the crystal surface can absorb oil, which can change its appearance. Use ritual oils, such as a few drops of an essential oil, along with a carrier oil such as jojoba or fractionated coconut oil or even olive oil. Applying oil to a crystal will change its appearance. Sometimes, this change accentuates the beauty of a crystal.

Charging Crystals

Once your crystals are clean and clear, they are ready to be charged. Charging your crystals is done through intention and touch. You keep a mental focus on the specific energy that you want to invoke or manifest, and you hold the crystal in your hands while you verbally speak your intention. The vibration of your voice will be received by the crystal and the universe. The crystal can then be used in spells, in charms, or on your altar. The steps of cleaning, clearing, and charging when done sequentially are a mediative ritual and a powerful exercise that will give you a bond with your crystals and strengthen your connection to them. This will improve your magickal abilities because difficult undertakings are often made manageable when you have the correct tool.

STORING AND DISPLAYING YOUR CRYSTALS

There are so many ways to store and display your crystals. You may find that you want only certain crystals visible at certain times. You may want them for ambient decor as well as spiritual tools on your altar. It is likely that you will not use and display all of the crystals in your collection at all times, so it is recommended that you explore the different options for different purposes and different times of the year, as well as which crystals can be in proximity to each other and which ones are best stored separately. The most important considerations for storing your crystals are that you are able to keep them dry, cool, and dust-free as well as secure while allowing for ease of handling.

Recommendations for Storage

The most important consideration for storing a crystal collection is keeping your crystals away from heat. This means they should not be in front of a window that receives direct sunlight for a long period of time. Also, they should not be near a radiator or heating vent. While it is true that crystals are formed under conditions of intense heat, certain crystals such as opal contain trace elements of water, and being regularly exposed to heat will have a detrimental effect on their appearance. Furthermore, direct sunlight can and will impact the color of crystals. It is fine to use the sun to charge a crystal when you acquire it, but exposing your crystals to direct sunlight on a regular basis is not recommended. Many crystals, dyed crystals in particular, are not color stable to begin with, and heat will only accelerate the degradation of color.

Avoiding Dust

Dust is another entity that you want to avoid, especially if your collection contains crystal clusters. Dust can settle in all the crevices and inclusions and make the crystal appear dull and lifeless. Crystals that are not on display can be stored in labeled boxes or pouches so that they remain bright, clean, and dust-free.

Another storage concern is safety. Crystals can be delicate. Fine points and corners can easily be chipped. You also want to protect your collection from theft, which is another consideration. How visible is your crystal collection in relation to the people around you, and are the people around you known or unknown? Be judicious about how you protect your crystals, particularly if you have rare and valuable crystals.

Labeling

If you plan to collect a variety of crystals, you will undoubtedly want a labeling system. You can do this in your grimoire by noting the distinct characteristics of each crystal you have, describing its color, size, and mineral type. A lot of crystals are very similar in appearance. Take sodalite and lapis lazuli, for example. To the untrained eye, these two crystals can appear very similar, having a similar hue and saturation of blue as well as some likeness in their color zoning and variegated color patterns, which can appear flecked in both crystals. Fluorite is another example. It occurs in such a wide range of colors, it could be confusing to distinguish lavender fluorite from amethyst or the green variety of fluorite from green tourmaline. Making notes or small labels for your crystals until they are familiar to you will help keep you from getting them mixed up. You may acquire a new crystal and believe that you will remember its mineral type, only to find you have forgotten and need to identify it again. Keeping a quick crystal inventory in your grimoire is an excellent way to organize your crystals. If you keep them stored in a consistent place, you can label the place where they belong, keeping your collection up-to-date and organized.

Storage Suggestions

A few suggestions for how to incorporate storage and display simultaneously include:

- **Curio cabinets.** Curio cabinets are small shelves enclosed in glass that will keep your collection visible and protected. You can affix labels to the shelves where the crystals belong.
- **An altar table with a drawer.** When you use crystals for a spiritual purpose, you will include them on your altar with intention. Any crystals that are unrelated to the spell at hand can be safely tucked away in a drawer. Using drawer dividers and lining the drawer with a soft cloth such as felt is another good way to store and protect your collection.
- **Shelves.** A dedicated crystal display shelf can be incorporated into your room decor appropriately as long as it is accessible and can be

easily dusted periodically. A shelf can be very simple or very ornate. Shelves that resemble crescent moons, shelves contained within a circular frame, even shelves that resemble animals and insects are lovely ways to display crystals. When choosing a display, remember that an item of poor quality is always going to be cheaper than something well-made. Buying something of poor quality might not actually save you any money in the long run, especially if you have to replace it or replace crystals that are damaged because the shelf became unstable.

Arranging for Display

Arranging crystals for display is an art form. You will want to pay attention to things like color, scale, spacing, background, levels, and lighting. Placing crystals at varying heights can allow you to enjoy your collection of crystals even when they are not employed in your magickal arts. Crystal collecting can be somewhat addictive, and you may find that you seek out stones of a particular height or size in order to create visual harmony. The peaceful effect that visual harmony creates is a form of magick as well as art. A crystal collection arranged with care, thought, and planning will have a positive effect on your energy. You will create something pleasing to the eye that brings you joy and enhances your environment, bringing you into alignment with peace and fulfillment.

COLOR

When arranging crystals for color, make a strong choice and see where it leads you. For example, you may want to arrange your crystals from warm hues to cool, following the spectrum in order to create a rainbow effect. Alternately, you may want to create excitement by placing color opposites next to each other, such as pairing amethyst with citrine or carnelian with green aventurine. Crystal transparency is another consideration. You might want to keep your transparent crystals together, or you might want to intersperse transparent crystals with a few opaque stones to create visual contrast and excitement. Whether you choose colors that are adjacent to each other on the spectrum or take the opposite approach, observe the different ways that colors interact and choose the arrangement that is the most pleasing to you. The only important thing is that the decisions you make are intentional while knowing that you can rearrange at any time.

SCALE

Arranging crystals according to scale creates a pleasing array that can be invigorating to look at. Placing a crystal tower in the middle of a shelf and then flanking it with smaller clusters on each side and gradually placing smaller stones such as tumbled crystals beside the clusters is one way that you can play with scale. Using crystals of varying sizes and observing the effects of how those differences in scale play off of each other can emphasize their visual appeal. Using graduated sizes can create a lovely tapered effect. You can use graduated sizes to create an interesting horizontal array or to create depth. Place smaller crystals at the front and larger crystals toward the back so that you maximize the visible surfaces of your crystals.

SPACING

Your crystals might be attractive cozied up next to each other, or they may need some breathing room. The important thing about spacing is to consider safety and handling as well as the negative space in between your crystals. Crystals should be spaced with enough distance between them so that you are not in danger of knocking any of them over when you go to reach for any particular crystal.

BACKGROUND

Nothing can interfere with presentation and display more than the background. Stick with a neutral, light-colored background so that your crystals are not competing with their environment. If you are using an enclosed cabinet, such as a curio, you can easily create a neutral background with paper or cardstock. Measure the far wall of the shelf and cut a piece of neutral-colored paper and affix it to the back of the shelf (or to the wall if the cabinet is not enclosed).

LIGHTING

Since the way crystals interact with light is an intrinsic part of their magickal properties, it makes sense to put some thought, planning, and care into how you illuminate your crystal collection. Avoid the use of incandescent light in close proximity to your colored crystals because heat can degrade the color of a crystal. Larger crystals such as sizable clusters or towers may benefit from being lit from below. Consider acquiring a crystal stand with an LED light. These are not expensive and will allow your important crystals to be displayed in such a manner that their color and inclusions will look amazing.

CANDLES

Crystals and candles can work very well together provided that you are keeping them a few inches apart. When incorporating candles into your crystal display, there are several things to consider. Here are some dos and don'ts for using crystals and candles together:

- Do use an array of tea lights to illuminate your crystal clusters.
- Don't put crystals directly next to an open flame.
- Do allow for a distance of 2–3 inches between a candle and a crystal.
- Don't leave a lighted candle unattended.
- Do place a crystal sphere 2–3 inches in front of a lit votive candle.
- Don't place a lit candle on your crystal shelf if there is another shelf directly above it.
- Do use a taper candle to illuminate a crystal tower by placing the taper behind the tower.
- Don't allow wax to drip onto your crystals.

PART TWO

A LIBRARY OF CRYSTALS

In this part you will find a quick and easy reference for fifty-five types of crystals that will help you gain an understanding of how they can be used in magick. Crystals are organized alphabetically by their common name. You will find information about the mineral group of each crystal, their crystal system, and where they are commonly found. While crystals have many different applications that reflect, impact, and transform the human condition, the most prominent and widely accepted attributes and applications are described for you. The main focus of each crystal is provided, as well as additional information about their magickal properties. For example, some crystals will be described as healers or revealers or used for grounding or balance.

You will also learn about the many different uses that individual crystals are known for; however, this library does not describe every possible use. You may discover new associations of your own as you grow in your practice of magick, and your own intuition and experience should never be discounted.

If a certain type of crystal brings you a vibration of peace or strength, yet the library describes it as a crystal of awakening, these effects are not contradictory. One may be the result of another. For example, the crystal may awaken that feeling of strength or peace, depending on your personal needs and the energy surrounding your spells, rituals, and general interactions. If you are using a crystal in meditation, it is easy to see how a sense of calm may pervade because of the context of use, no matter what the ascribed magickal properties may be.

Agate

TUMBLED AGATE CRYSTAL

- **Crystal System:** Trigonal crystals with individual units that are so small they can only be seen with a microscope, if at all
- **Focus:** Balance and Grounding
- **Color Range:** Agate presents in an array of colors from colorless, gray, red, and white to blue, brown, ocher, yellow, and orange. Agate is often distinguished by its varied bands of color and is typically multicolored.
- **Characteristics:** A type of chalcedony, agate is relatively common and found throughout the world. Its bands of varying colors are usually translucent. Agate is frequently dyed to enhance its appearance and is often sold as tumbled stones, slices, or slabs.
- **Magickal Properties:** Agate is a stone of vitality. Representing the life force, agate is also a powerful stone for grounding. It can transform negative thought patterns even if they are deeply rooted. Agate is restorative and can replenish physical energy. It can increase your awareness of the connection among all living things. Agate can create balance between the body and the spirit. This is one of the main applications of its grounding qualities, imparting a sense of equilibrium between mind and body, body and spirit, and spirit and mind.
- **Crystal History:** The use of agate is ancient. It is believed that it was either first discovered or first described by the Greek philosopher Theophrastus and named for the Achates River. In the biblical book of Exodus and in rabbinical literature, agate is described as being used in the breastplate of the high priest, which is also referred to as the breastplate of judgment.

Amazonite

◀ ROUGH AND UNCUT AMAZONITE CRYSTAL CLUSTER

- **Crystal System:** Triclinic
- **Focus:** Connector, Revealer, and Protector
- **Color Range:** Green and bluish green with flecks of gray.
- **Characteristics:** Sometimes referred to as Amazon jade or Amazon stone, amazonite crystals have a blocky appearance and are generally seen in varying shades of bluish green. Although it is named for the Amazon River, there are no known discoveries of amazonite in that region. Amazonite is most frequently seen in the United States, Madagascar, Brazil, and Russia.
- **Magickal Properties:** Amazonite functions as both a revealer and a connector. It can help you connect to your true essence and aid in magick based on self-discovery. Amazonite can also help you connect your ideas and beliefs to your emotions, helping you understand why certain things may bother you. Amazonite is useful in spells because it can connect intentions to manifestations. A stone of truth and harmony, amazonite promotes inner freedom. Amazonite allows its bearer to receive spiritual messages and communications, making it extremely useful in divination. Amazonite is also used in deflecting conflict and in healing magick for those recovering from a traumatic experience. It can also be used protectively in order to guard against conflict altogether.
- **Crystal History:** Amazonite has a lengthy history dating back thousands of years and was used by ancient Sumerians and Babylonians in jewelry, talismans, and seals. Although amazonite is considered very ancient, the reason for its soothing blue-green color was discovered only recently. Most scientists had assumed amazonite's color was due to copper content in the feldspar, but now it is believed to be caused by trace amounts of lead.

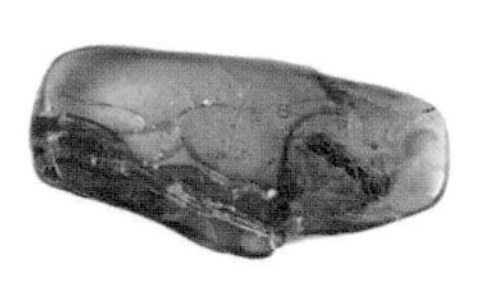

Amber

◀ NATURAL AND UNCUT AMBER

- **CRYSTAL SYSTEM:** None
- **FOCUS:** Transformer and Healer
- **COLOR RANGE:** Yellow to golden yellow, golden brown, and brown.
- **CHARACTERISTICS:** Because of its organic nature, amber is not a mineral and has no consistent lattice arrangement of atoms. Amber is a form of petrified tree resin found in a variety of places, including northern and eastern Europe as well as the United Kingdom. Amber is millions of years old and has been known to contain other organic matter such as fossilized insects or plant material. Amber can also pick up static charges of electricity when rubbed across a surface such as fur. This led the Greeks to refer to it as "electrum."
- **MAGICKAL PROPERTIES:** Amber has associations with wealth, health, protection, and manifesting. Its golden hue makes it ideal for spells invoking prosperity and abundance. There is also a modern practice of sewing buttons made of amber onto clothing to protect loved ones, particularly the elderly, from ill health. Amber instills a sense of comfort. Amber is a time traveler from the far distant past, coming into being when a tree is so abundant with resin that it overflows. This is another characteristic that makes it suitable for spells of increase. And because it essentially changes form, amber is a powerful gem that can aid manifestation magick when you need a major transmutation to occur.
- **CRYSTAL HISTORY:** Amber is a fascinating gem, and although it is not a true crystal, its origin and unique characteristics make it ideally suited for magick. It was revered by the Norse as well as the Romans, who believed it had the power to bestow immortality. Gladiators would wear it into battle as a protective charm.

Amethyst

TUMBLED AMETHYST CRYSTAL

- **Crystal System:** Trigonal
- **Focus:** Awakener
- **Color Range:** Pale lavender to deep purple.
- **Characteristics:** Amethyst grows in basalt, forming clusters contained within geodes (pockets of rock). Amethyst gets its enchanting purple hues from trace amounts of iron that are present in its crystalline lattice. The hexagonal structure appears as a six-sided pyramid with varying sizes of amethyst crystals growing close to each other. Frequently short and stubby, amethyst also grows in longer crystals, but these are rare.
- **Magickal Properties:** Amethyst is considered one of the most powerful gems, largely due to its color and crystal structure. Amethyst aligns with the crown chakra, which is the highest level of spiritual awareness and actualization. For this reason, wearing amethyst on or around the head is auspicious. For an accomplished witch, this means embedding amethyst in a crown or diadem or even a headband. For those seeking to achieve a higher state of spiritual awareness and receive oracular messages, amethyst earrings would be an appropriate choice. Amethyst is also associated with healing properties. The number three is considered sacred because it represents the three aspects of the goddess. Since amethyst originates as a six-sided crystal, this powerful association is doubled.
- **Crystal History:** Ancient Romans believed that amethyst was a potent antidote to alcohol overconsumption. Amethyst was once considered a precious gemstone, prized along with rubies, sapphires, emeralds, and diamonds. It wasn't until vast amethyst deposits were discovered in the early 1800s in Brazil that amethyst became accessible to all.

Ametrine

TUMBLED AMETRINE CRYSTAL

- **Crystal System:** Trigonal
- **Focus:** Uniter
- **Color Range:** Ametrine is a variety of quartz that shows the color range of both amethyst and citrine in a single crystal. Its two-toned appearance ranges from golden yellow to purple.
- **Characteristics:** Ametrine is essentially two different gems occurring in the same crystal. The contrasting hues of honey and lavender give ametrine its appeal. It is a visually stimulating bicolor stone. Like amethyst and citrine, it grows mainly in short, stubby clusters. Ametrine is found only in Bolivia. It is characterized by its dramatic and distinct color zones.
- **Magickal Properties:** Ametrine is a stone of union and discovery. It can bridge gaps in communication, link new awakenings to spiritual ascension, and heal divides. Ametrine can unite seemingly different parts of yourself, allowing you to embrace the wholeness of your being. While you may be many different things to different people, ametrine allows you to explore these differences and the beauty that can result from acceptance. Ametrine is also a crystal that can be used for invoking love and blossoming relationships. Ametrine has been used to enhance clairvoyant abilities and to harmonize the body and spirit.
- **Crystal History:** Originally discovered in the 1600s, ametrine is associated with royalty. Legends and lore surrounding ametrine claim it was discovered in Bolivia by a conquistador who named the mine Anahí after his princess. The location of the ametrine mine was then lost for three hundred years, and no further records of ametrine were discovered until the 1900s. Legends state that ametrine was revered by pre-Columbian people before the conquistador Don Felipe de Urriola Goita carried it to Spain and gifted it to the queen.

Apatite

◀ ROUGH AND UNCUT SKY BLUE APATITE CRYSTAL

- **Crystal System:** Hexagonal
- **Focus:** Revealer
- **Color Range:** Apatite has a strong resemblance to beryl, quartz, and fluorite. It occurs in many colors, including green, purple, pink, white, yellow, and sky blue. Apatite can also be fluorescent.
- **Characteristics:** Because of its appearance, apatite is often confused with other minerals, most notably beryl, quartz, and fluorite. For this reason, its name is derived from the Greek word for "deceive." It was discovered and named in 1788 by the German geologist Abraham Werner and is found in Brazil, Myanmar, Switzerland, Czech Republic, Slovakia, Italy, Bolivia, Mexico, and Maine, which produces the variety of deepest purple. It is sometimes referred to as "fake beryl." It can also contain rutiles, giving certain stones the "cat's eye" effect known as chatoyancy. Apatite is composed of the same mineral that makes up teeth and bone.
- **Magickal Properties:** Apatite is a stone of inspiration, growth, and psychic enhancement. It is also known as the revealer of truth. When obfuscation or dishonesty arises, apatite can be used to uncover the truth of the matter. It is a powerful stone that can be used to silence gossip or to help a person prevail in court. Apatite is also used in animal magick because of its chemical resemblance to teeth and bones. Apatite can be used to manifest a familiar.
- **Crystal History:** For a long time, apatite defied classification because of its similar appearance to other crystals. Apatite does not have a long history of use because it wasn't scientifically identified until the late 1700s. It does have some remarkable properties and applications due to its unique composition. Apatite has been used in everything from ceramics to prosthetics.

Apophyllite

◀ NATURAL APOPHYLLITE CRYSTAL CLUSTER

- **Crystal System:** Tetragonal
- **Focus:** Connector and Revealer
- **Color Range:** Clear and colorless to white, and rarely yellow, green, and pink.
- **Characteristics:** Apophyllite has a unique luster that adds to its appeal. Its name is used to refer to three mineral types that all share similar chemistry and characteristics: fluorapophyllite (the most common), hydroxyapophyllite, and natroapophyllite (the least common), but are all commonly referred to as just apophyllite. Apophyllite crystals tend to be very large and also very well formed, making them attractive to crystal collectors. The most significant apophyllite discoveries have been in India, specifically in the region known as the Deccan Traps.
- **Magickal Properties:** Apophyllite is considered a crystal that has the ability to connect its user to the spiritual realm. Apophyllite is used in meditation and can assist those who are seeking to engage in astral travel. The crystal has very distinct triangular corners and is often double terminated, hence its reputed use as a bridge to the spirit world. When placed over the third eye, apophyllite acts as a revealer, illuminating truth and stimulating energy. It is a consciousness opener.
- **Crystal History:** Apophyllite gets its name from its primary characteristics. It stems from the Greek words "apo" and "phyllos," meaning "away from" and "leaf," respectively. Because of its high water content, apophyllite tends to flake apart when it is exposed to heat. These flakes appear like small leaves cleaving off of the crystal surface. Apophyllite has a beautiful subtle luster and is often transparent, giving it an otherworldly sheen. It was officially named in 1806 by René Just-Haüy.

Aquamarine

◀ NATURAL AND UNCUT AQUAMARINE CRYSTAL

- **Crystal System:** Hexagonal
- **Focus:** Protection and Healing
- **Color Range:** Aquamarine is transparent, making it one of the rarer and more desirable types of crystals. It is naturally a pale blue to blue-green.
- **Characteristics:** Traces of iron impart the sea green color that aquamarine is known for. Aquamarine is sometimes heat treated because the application of heat reduces the green overtones, resulting in a purer blue color. Aquamarine is found primarily in granite pegmatites and metamorphic rocks that have been worn away by erosion. It has been unearthed in Brazil, Italy, Ireland, Austria, Russia, and locations in and around the Ural Mountains. In the United States, aquamarine has been found in Massachusetts, Colorado, and California.
- **Magickal Properties:** Aquamarine is a healing stone that also protects its bearer from harm. Associated with the sea, aquamarine allows you to tap into the depths of your emotions and experience tranquility and calm. Aquamarine can be used to usher in a new beginning, especially any new state of affairs that comes into play after an upset. Aquamarine can also counter feelings of being overwhelmed. It is a calming stone and an opener that can be used to bolster courage and strength.
- **Crystal History:** Aquamarine has a long and illustrious history. Due to its color, it was heavily associated with protection, particularly from storms at sea. It was frequently carried by Roman fishermen as a talisman of safety. Aquamarine was even prescribed by ancient doctors as a cure for bloating. Aquamarine was desired and admired by many ancient cultures, including Sumerian, Babylonian, Egyptian, and Greek. In the Bible, it is considered one of the emblems of the apostle St. Thomas.

Aragonite

◀ NATURAL UNCUT ARAGONITE CRYSTAL

- **Crystal System:** Orthorhombic
- **Focus:** Grounding and Stabilizing
- **Color Range:** Golden orange, red and yellow, gray, green, blue and even colorless or white.
- **Characteristics:** Aragonite is a polymorph, meaning that it has the same chemical composition of calcium carbonate but a different crystal structure. It is relatively rare compared to other crystals because it forms only under high-pressure conditions. When aragonite is exposed to heat, it can spontaneously change into calcite. Aragonite can also dissolve when exposed to water for a long amount of time.
- **Magickal Properties:** Aragonite is useful for shifting energy or anytime you need to move from one thing to another; for example, from chaos to calm or from the material plane to the astral plane. A crystal of balance, aragonite can be used to calm and heal the emotions, increase strength and stamina, and bring the self into alignment with love. Aragonite is also a clearing crystal and can be used in aura cleansing to rid the energetic field surrounding the body of negative energy. Aragonite has been used to quell anger and transform energy. It is extremely useful during times of stress due to its ability to ground physical energy. Use aragonite when you need to develop patience and remain grounded, particularly during times of change. Aragonite is a stone of balance, healing, patience, and growth.
- **Crystal History:** A fascinating aspect of aragonite is its absence from certain types of sedimentary rock because of how it reacts with water. Discovered in 1797, it is rarely seen in the geologic record. In the rare instances that is does appear, aragonite is considered very important to the geological record because it occurs in meteorites and appears to be able to survive indefinitely on a scale of millions to billions of years as long as it remains separated from water.

Aventurine

TUMBLED AVENTURINE CRYSTAL

- **Crystal System:** Triclinic
- **Focus:** Inspiration, Growth, Wealth, and Luck
- **Color Range:** Pale to dark green, blue, yellow, white, and reddish brown.
- **Characteristics:** Flecks of mica give aventurine its distinctive sparkle. This unique characteristic is referred to as aventurescence. Usually green, aventurine is a semi-translucent crystal, which makes its appearance somewhat similar to certain varieties of jade. Sometimes aventurine is referred to as "Indian jade," which is a misnomer although significant deposits of aventurine have been discovered in India as well as Brazil and Austria. Aventurine is often dyed very bright colors.
- **Magickal Properties:** Aventurine is a crystal of inspiration. It can activate creativity and usher in periods of creative growth. Aventurine can be used to heal the heart and open a witch to new possibilities pertaining to love and fortune. Intensely positive, aventurine is used to promote good luck and fortune, happiness, productivity, success, and expansion. It is also useful in healing matters of the heart.
- **Crystal History:** Aventurine gets its name from the Corsican phrase "a ventura," which loosely translates to "the fortune." It is also connected to the Italian "avventura," meaning "adventure" or "by chance." According to Renaissance lore, the optical phenomenon of aventurescence was accidentally discovered in the 1600s by Italian glassmakers who created a similar effect by unintentionally contaminating molten glass with copper particles, mimicking the metallic sparkle that aventurine naturally exhibits.

Azurite

◀ ROUGH AND UNCUT AZURITE CRYSTAL

- **CRYSTAL SYSTEM:** Monoclinic
- **FOCUS:** Communicator and Transformer
- **COLOR RANGE:** Deep royal blue to azure blue and dark blue.
- **CHARACTERISTICS:** Uncommon and captivating, azurite is an extremely attractive ornamental crystal owing to its intense blue saturation. Azurite is rare and occurs only under certain conditions that require the presence of water containing dissolved copper particles by way of a reaction with carbonic acid. Striations of various shades of deep blue are common, giving azurite a strong visual association with the ocean. Azurite is also a pseudomorph and can change to malachite. Azurite and malachite are frequently found together.
- **MAGICKAL PROPERTIES:** Azurite is a crystal highly suited to improving relationships and heightening psychic abilities. By producing a calming state, azurite opens the door to communication and allows the third eye to engage. Useful for balancing the emotions, azurite can also be used to transform situations and relationships in order to move them into the direction you want. If you want information and insight together with a calm but heightened awareness, azurite crystals are an effective aid to bring about this state of mind.
- **CRYSTAL HISTORY:** Azurite has been in use since ancient times in a variety of ways. It has been ground into a pigment, used for adornment, and exploited for its copper content. From ancient Egypt to the Middle Ages, azurite was important for its use in painting; however, its use was eventually supplanted by synthetics. This was mainly due to azurite's nature as a pseudomorph. It faded and even changed color over time.

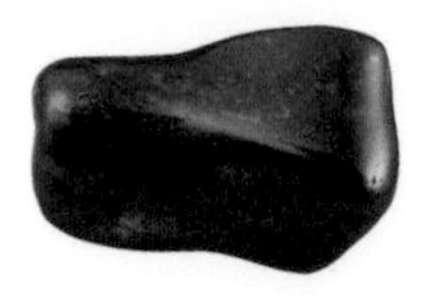

Bloodstone

TUMBLED BLOODSTONE CRYSTAL

- **Crystal System:** Trigonal with individual units that can only be seen with a microscope
- **Focus:** Healing, Purification, and Renewal
- **Color Range:** Dark green or bluish green with flecks of red.
- **Characteristics:** Bloodstone is the common name for heliotrope (not to be confused with the flowering plant that shares the same name), which is an aggregation of minerals including quartz and chalcedony or jasper. Its appearance is variegated, and although it is usually a deep green, it is characterized by a spattering of bright red interspersed throughout the lattice. Most bloodstone comes from India. Bloodstone is a durable stone and is most often seen as tumbled crystals or cut into cabochons.
- **Magickal Properties:** Bloodstone has strong associations with courage. It is used to overcome obstacles and clear paths in business and legal work due to its ability to strengthen the mind. Its qualities of renewal are connected to its effectiveness in removing fear that causes blocks to success. Because of its appearance, bloodstone reminds one of the importance of vitality: Just as blood carries oxygen to one's cells, bloodstone helps renew depleted spiritual energy. Bloodstone is useful anytime you need to face a fear, overcome an obstacle, or get a needed energy lift.
- **Magickal History:** In the Middle Ages, bloodstone was often used in religious carvings depicting Jesus Christ or Mary the Virgin Mother and carried great significance. It came to be associated with martyrdom due to the red spotting resulting from iron oxides, which create the "drops of blood" effect. In 1879, bloodstone was recorded as the birthstone for March in a book called *A Christmas Ring*, which described bloodstone's association with courage, immortality, and victory.

Carnelian

◀ TUMBLED CARNELIAN CRYSTAL

- **CRYSTAL SYSTEM:** Trigonal with individual units that can only be seen with a microscope
- **FOCUS:** Stabilizer and Restorer
- **COLOR RANGE:** Red to reddish brown and orange.
- **CHARACTERISTICS:** Carnelian is a variety of chalcedony and is often seen with striated bands and color zones that range from red to orange.
- **MAGICKAL PROPERTIES:** Carnelian is used for grounding and cleansing, particularly for cleansing and attuning other types of crystals. It has a stabilizing energy, and for this reason, carnelian acts as a restorer: It can amplify vitality and motivation while stimulating creativity. Because of its ruddy color, carnelian is strongly associated with the life force. As a talisman, carnelian can bring hope, comfort, and protection. Carnelian is universally considered to be an auspicious crystal, associated with good fortune, power, courage, spirituality, and royalty.
- **CRYSTAL HISTORY:** Carnelian has long been considered a very important crystal. In the ancient past, carnelian was referred to as a stone of kings and was even worn by the prophet Muhammad, who was described as having a carnelian ring set in silver. Napoleon carried a carved carnelian talisman with him into battle and later gifted it to his son, suggesting that the ruler believed in its power to influence events.

Celestite

◀ NATURAL CELESTITE CLUSTER

- **Crystal System:** Orthorhombic
- **Focus:** Ascension, Calming, and Connecting
- **Color Range:** Light blue, white, and colorless.
- **Characteristics:** Celestite, also called celestine, is a relatively soft crystal and owes its name to its pale blue color. Named for the Latin term "caelestis," which means "heavenly," celestite is often associated with angels, the sky, and celestial energy. Notable deposits of celestite, a type of strontium mineral, have been found in Italy, Spain, Madagascar, Canada, and the United States. Celestite flakes are used in fireworks because they emit a bright red color when ignited.
- **Magickal Properties:** Celestite is often used in healing because of its association with purity, angels, and the celestial realm. Celestite is believed to open a link to the angels and make the heavens accessible. This means that celestite can bring about a sense of peace and calm. It is used to address fears and phobias and promote serenity. Innocence, lightness of being, and spiritual ascension are all states that celestite is used to amplify.
- **Crystal History:** Celestite crystals were discovered in Italy, but they were not correctly identified until the 1780s. It wasn't until the discovery of the element strontium in 1790 that celestite lost some of its mystery because strontium is a part of celestite. Without the strontium element, celestite would otherwise just bear a strong resemblance to barite and it wouldn't be as unique.

Chalcedony

TUMBLED BLUE LACE CHALCEDONY

- **Crystal System:** Trigonal with individual units that can only be seen with a microscope
- **Focus:** Harmonizer and Nurturer
- **Color Range:** Pale blue, green, white, or gray.
- **Characteristics:** Chalcedony is a type of quartz with a translucent appearance and a luster that can be described as waxy. When chalcedony presents with banded striations that are pale blue, it is called blue lace agate. Chalcedony is filled with microscopic quartz crystals.
- **Magickal Properties:** Chalcedony is a stone of friendship. It promotes kindness, goodwill, and harmony. Chalcedony is particularly useful in coven craft, as it has an ability to contribute to feelings of serenity and help mediate emotions in groups. Chalcedony helps you discern the subtleties in group relationships, leading to balance and understanding. In addition to covens, chalcedony is also a great crystal for the workplace, school, or other situations where success is dependent upon other people. It is grounding for both the heart and the mind.
- **Crystal History:** Discovered in Turkey, chalcedony is a descriptor for a large group of silicate minerals including agate, jasper, heliotrope or bloodstone, and carnelian, but the name is most synonymous with the light blue and sometimes banded variety. In the 1500s, Georgius Agricola, known as "the father of minerology," described a stone believed to be chalcedony because it was named for the district of Chalcedon in modern Istanbul.

Charoite

◀ ROUGH AND UNCUT CHAROITE CRYSTAL

- **Crystal System:** Monoclinic
- **Focus:** Transformer and Revealer
- **Color Range:** Most commonly exhibits violet, lilac, and brown hues with a white or whitish gray marbled effect.
- **Characteristics:** Recently discovered in the Siberian regions of Russia, charoite is known for the swirling effect visible in its purplish color bands. Charoite quickly became associated with magick due to its relative rarity and its lilac color and unique signature patterns. Often exhibiting a spinning spiral pattern, charoite is considered compatible with opening the crown chakra.
- **Magickal Properties:** Charoite is strongly associated with transformations. It is also considered a revealer of mysteries. If you aren't sure which path you should be on, working with charoite can help you determine what your next steps should be. Charoite is a ward against negativity. It is used in protective magick and in healing traumas from a past life that can carry over and affect you in your current life. Charoite is also associated with service, making it useful for coven leaders in witchcraft.
- **Crystal History:** Discovered in the 1970s, charoite is believed by some people to be named for the Chara River in Siberia; however, this seems unlikely due to the location of the river and the place of discovery. The name is considered a reference to the Russian word "ocharovaniye" (meaning "charm").

Chrysoberyl

◀ ROUGH AND UNCUT CHRYSOBERYL CRYSTAL

- **Crystal System:** Orthorhombic
- **Focus:** Empowering and Attaining Resolution and Insight
- **Color Range:** Yellow to green, yellowish green, greenish brown to brown and blue.
- **Characteristics:** Chrysoberyl is best known for its "cat's eye" effect. Parallel rutile fibers create the thin line of reflected light that makes this crystal appear similar to the vertical pupil of felines. Some varieties of chrysoberyl can also change color when viewed under different types of light. In spite of its name, chrysoberyl is not part of the beryl group of crystals.
- **Magickal Properties:** Chrysoberyl is often used for healing in relationships. It is said to enhance insight, and, as such, is useful whenever you find yourself at a crossroads or you are confronting a particularly difficult decision. Chrysoberyl will help you examine multiple sides of an issue and help lead you to the best possible outcome for all involved. A stone of clarity and forgiveness, chrysoberyl is a powerful emotional healer that will help you see situations fairly.
- **Crystal History:** Named for the Greek words for "golden" and "beryl," chrysoberyl was first discovered in 1789. Unearthed in a Russian emerald mine, alexandrite is a rare, valuable, and fascinating variety of chrysoberyl. Named after the czar's oldest son, alexandrite was discovered in 1830 on his twelfth birthday and is remarkable because under candlelight, it appears red, while in daylight, it appears green. These were incidentally the same colors as those of the Russian Imperial Guard.

Chrysocolla

CUT AND POLISHED CHRYSOCOLLA SPHERE

- **Crystal System:** Orthorhombic
- **Focus:** Healer
- **Color Range:** Bluish green with concentrated areas of blue and green color, often seen with white and brown flecks. Bearing a strong resemblance to turquoise, chrysocolla has a high copper content and a waxy surface appearance.
- **Characteristics:** Chrysocolla has been used since ancient times in jewelry, but not in the way that you might expect. Because of the copper present in its chemical composition, chrysocolla was often ground into fine powder and used to solder gold.
- **Magickal Properties:** Chrysocolla is a crystal of rejuvenation, empowerment, and improvement in communication. A powerful healer, it is a bridge between receiving and accepting love and demonstrating and communicating love. Chrysocolla is a stone of truth and authenticity. It helps you tap into your innate wisdom and honest desires while giving you the strength to express them clearly. Its early use as a binding agent reveals its natural ability to join, heal, and preserve connections.
- **Crystal History:** Known since ancient times, chrysocolla is named for the Greek words for "gold" and "glue." Theophrastus was the first to describe chrysocolla around 300 B.C.E. It was regarded as a stone of wisdom.

Citrine

◀ ROUGH AND UNCUT CITRINE CRYSTAL

- **Crystal System:** Trigonal
- **Focus:** Manifesting Success and Positivity
- **Color Range:** Golden yellow to pale yellow and brownish orange.
- **Characteristics:** Trace amounts of iron give citrine its sunny color. If citrine is a pale yellow, it is referred to as lemon quartz. Sometimes, citrine is created by heat treating amethyst.
- **Magickal Properties:** A powerful mood lifter, citrine radiates success and positivity. Citrine is additionally associated with wellness and material comfort. It is also used in psychic healing and in activating personal will and initiative. When you come from a place of balance and peace, manifesting specific objectives is easier, and citrine is an ideal crystal for accomplishing this. Its golden hues can instill a heightened sense of confidence and ability. Citrine is a crystal for leaders, movers, and shakers. It is a powerful stone for actualization and can strengthen a person's aura. Citrine is an especially cheerful crystal.
- **Crystal History:** Citrine is a crystal for the ages. It appears in ancient lore from Egyptian to classical Greek and Roman. Citrine was believed to augment wealth, bring desire into being, assuage anger, and restore goodwill.

Emerald

◀ ROUGH AND UNCUT EMERALD CRYSTALS

- **Crystal System:** Hexagonal
- **Focus:** Prognosticator and Revealer of Truth
- **Color Range:** Intense green to bluish green.
- **Characteristics:** Emeralds are a relatively soft gemstone known for their alluring internal inclusions. Transparent emeralds are rare and extremely expensive, but emerald crystals of lesser quality are quite accessible. Trace amounts of chromium in beryl create an emerald, and beryl is described as emerald only when the color green is intensely saturated. Emeralds are found only in a few places in the world such as Colombia, Afghanistan, Russia, and Zambia.
- **Magickal Properties:** Emeralds are associated with love, healing, abundance, and compassion. Emerald is heart opening and heart healing. It can impact relationships at all levels: new, established, or transitioning. Emerald invites you to explore your emotions in a safe way. It is also used in magick for prosperity and abundance. And emeralds are used in divination, to uncover deception, and to foretell future events.
- **Crystal History:** Dating back to 1500 B.C.E., the Egyptians were among the first to discover the captivating beauty of emeralds. Emerald was considered a gem of queens; Cleopatra famously had an emerald collection. Ancient cultures held the belief that an emerald allowed a person to get a glimpse of the future if the gem was placed under the tongue and held there. Additionally, emeralds were considered to have protective magick.

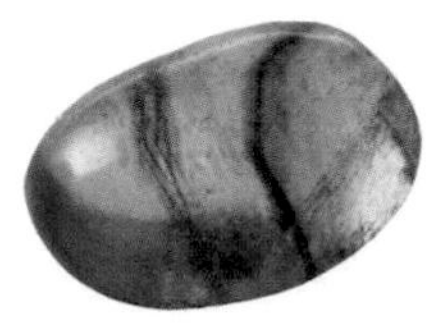

Fluorite

◀ TUMBLED FLUORITE CRYSTAL

- **Crystal System:** Cubic
- **Focus:** Ascension and Flow
- **Color Range:** Fluorite occurs in a wide spectrum of colors, including pale blue, blue-green, from light green to dark green, yellow, brown, purple and violets to gray, black, and clear. The most unusual and rarest of all the colors of fluorite are pink and red.
- **Characteristics:** Brightly colored, fluorite exhibits fluorescence, meaning it will glow under ultraviolet light. In fact, fluorescence is so named because of fluorite. When the color of fluorite runs parallel to the crystal face, this is considered a very desirable characteristic. Fluorite has been discovered in a variety of European countries such as England, Germany, the Czech Republic, and Slovakia. Additionally, fluorite occurs in Mexico and Ontario, and in the United States it has been found in Illinois, Ohio, New York, and Arizona.
- **Magickal Properties:** Fluorite has been called a "fairyland" crystal, owing mostly to its brilliant spectrum of colors, especially the pink variety, which occurs in granite. When you are feeling depleted, fluorite can act as a restorative crystal. It is both energizing and uplifting. Fluorite can be used to overcome obstacles and accelerate spiritual awakenings. Traditionally powerful with unique properties, fluorite has the ability to glow, which makes it applicable to accessing unseen frequencies and amplifying your psychic awareness. It is also used in decision-making and improving focus.
- **Crystal History:** Fluorite was discovered in the sixteenth century by Georgius Agricola. Its name is derived from the Latin word "fluere," meaning "flow," due to its use in glassmaking. Early miners of fluorite discovered that it could change color when viewed under different light conditions. Used in etching in addition to glassmaking, fluorite was also used for carving in Asian countries such as Japan and China.

Garnet

ROUGH AND UNCUT GARNET CRYSTAL

- **CRYSTAL SYSTEM:** Cubic
- **FOCUS:** Vitality and Passion
- **COLOR RANGE:** Red, reddish brown, and black.
- **CHARACTERISTICS:** Garnet is most commonly seen in reds, but depending on what trace elements it contains, garnet can present in a variety of colors, which are then all given specific names, such as spessartite (orangey red), rhodolite (rosy red), and tsavorite (bright green).
- **MAGICKAL PROPERTIES:** If you need motivation, garnet is an excellent crystal to work with. Garnet is a revitalizing stone and is also used for purification and balancing energy. It can inflame passion and inspire love and devotion, but it also carries an association with serenity. Garnet is useful in long-term relationships and for elevating existing relationships to a more serious nature.
- **CRYSTAL HISTORY:** Garnet has been known since the Bronze Age and has been a part of human consciousness for at least five thousand years. Its name is derived from the Latin word for "pomegranate," "granatium." During the Middle Ages, garnet was worn by high-ranking clergy and nobles. Garnet was worn by Romans in signet rings and was sometimes referred to as "carbuncle." It was considered a gift from God bestowed to the biblical king Solomon. Egyptian pharaohs were buried with garnet necklaces and other adornments.

Heliodor

◀ ROUGH AND UNCUT HELIODOR CRYSTAL

- **Crystal System:** Hexagonal
- **Crystal Focus:** Renewal and Awakening
- **Color Range:** Light to golden yellow.
- **Characteristics:** While beryl is naturally colorless like many crystals, trace amounts of iron transform clear beryl into heliodor. Heliodor is often transparent and is occasionally known by the misnomer "yellow emerald" because emerald and heliodor are both beryl group minerals. Heliodor has been found in Brazil, Ukraine, Russia, and parts of the United States, including Maine and Connecticut.
- **Magickal Properties:** Sunny, golden, and transparent, heliodor is a stone that invites happiness and new beginnings. Associated with the sun, heliodor warms relationships, particularly familial relationships, and is used in spells of wealth and abundance. Heliodor opens the heart to unexpected pleasures. Use heliodor when you need to be replenished, energized, and awakened to new possibilities.
- **Crystal History:** Heliodor was discovered in 1912 in what is now Namibia, making it a rather recent discovery when compared to other crystals; however, as part of the beryl group, this family of crystals has been known for a very long time. Its name is derived from the Greek words "ílios," meaning "sun," and "dóro," meaning "gift." Many gemologists consider it distinct from golden beryl, which has a greater saturation of yellow.

Hematite

TUMBLED HEMATITE CRYSTAL

- **Crystal System:** Trigonal
- **Focus:** Grounding and Protection
- **Color Range:** Gray, red, and brown.
- **Characteristics:** Hematite commonly occurs in steely gray colors with a distinct metallic luster. Hematite is named for its effect of leaving a red, blood-like streak when scratched against a surface. Abundant in North America, Brazil, Venezuela, and Canada, hematite also has magnetic properties. There is considerable excitement surrounding hematite, as it is believed to also exist on the planet Mars, according to recent data reported by NASA from the Mars Exploration Rovers mission.
- **Magickal Properties:** Hematite is frequently used for grounding energy, dispelling negativity, and offering protection, as well as in divination. It can promote sleep and restore energy. It has a power to attract and is said to absorb negative energy and return it to the earth. Hematite is also used for protection of the home and of the psyche. It is used in hex breaking and to ward off psychic attacks.
- **Crystal History:** Hematite has been recognized since around 300 B.C.E. Called "bloodstone" by Theophrastus, its name has evolved over the centuries, but all variations are connected to blood. In the year 79, the Roman naturalist Pliny the Elder described the stone as "haematite," which is connected to the Greek word "haimatites," meaning "blood-like." Its use as a pigment is staggeringly ancient, dating back to prehistoric times. Hematite residue has been found in graves believed to be 64,000–80,000 years old. It seems that hematite has been intertwined with human expression from time immemorial.

Iolite

ROUGH AND UNCUT IOLITE CRYSTAL

- **Crystal System:** Orthorhombic
- **Focus:** Balance and Focus
- **Color Range:** Cornflower blue to violet.
- **Characteristics:** Iolite (also known as cordierite) is sometimes known as the "water sapphire." As a crystal, iolite can exhibit pleochroism, meaning that it will appear differently when viewed from different angles. It can look as clear as water or as vivid as a sapphire.
- **Magickal Properties:** Iolite is useful for focusing and returning to a state of balance. It is also useful in overcoming the feeling of being overwhelmed, and it helps promote clarity and organization. Iolite is wonderful when used alongside crystals for prosperity and abundance such as pyrite and aventurine, as iolite is useful during times when responsibilities are growing. It is a confidence builder and can be a source of strength and endurance during unfamiliar or otherwise trying circumstances. Iolite can be helpful in overcoming disorganized habits, helping you look at situations from different points of view, and determining the next steps on your journey.
- **Crystal History:** Named for Pierre Cordier, who discovered the mineral cordierite, more commonly known as iolite, this crystal was once confused for tanzanite due to its violet blue color. Discovered in Spain in 1815, iolite has been connected to unverified legends that Vikings used it as a navigational aid because its ability to polarize light helped Viking sailors determine the position of the sun on cloudy days.

Jade

◀ TRANSLUCENT TUMBLED JADE CRYSTAL

- **Crystal System:** Monoclinic
- **Focus:** Vitality and Wisdom
- **Color Range:** Deep olivine to pale green, also pale blue, yellow, and white. Translucent pale green is the most highly sought-after variety of jade.
- **Characteristics:** Jade has several characteristics that make it desirable. Its smooth and sleek surface and translucence give jade an ethereal quality. Although jade comes in almost every color, the deep translucent green variety is considered the most desirable and is known as Imperial jade. There are two types of jade that are considered valuable: jadeite and nephrite. Jadeite is the rarer of the two. Jade is considered to be an ornamental gem due to its translucence and ability to be easily carved.
- **Magickal Properties:** Jade is associated with strengthening the heart as well as the emotional and physical selves. Jade can be used when you need to feel more receptive to joy. Jade represents attainment in the material world, as well as maturity and wisdom. The joy that it inspires comes from within, and not solely from the trappings of wealth. Jade is considered a stone of luck and good fortune. It can aid in making wise decisions surrounding money.
- **Crystal History:** Jade has a rich and illustrative history that dates back three thousand years. There is a whole artistic tradition of jade carving that remains popular today. Jade carvings have specific associations, and recurring motifs have cultural meanings, particularly across Asia. Jade bats are associated with happiness, while butterflies symbolize longevity. A jade dragon is a symbol of power. A jade peach represents eternal life. There is also the symbol of the bi. The bi is a round disc with a hole in the center, which is a symbol of the realm of heaven.

Jasper

◀ TUMBLED JASPER CRYSTAL

- **Crystal System:** Trigonal with individual units that can only be seen under magnification
- **Focus:** Strength and Power
- **Color Range:** Jasper most often occurs in the color red. It is rarely uniform in color and can present in earth tones, including brown, yellow, and green.
- **Characteristics:** Opaque and often spotted or banded with various colors, jasper is known by many names, several of which pertain to the variety and pattern of colors. Bloodstone, leopard, and mookaite are some of the common names for jasper. When exhibiting colorful bands, it is referred to as picture jasper or landscape jasper. Jasper is relatively stable, not particularly rare, and is often used in carving. It is a type of chalcedony with a microcrystalline structure.
- **Magickal Properties:** Jasper has powerful properties that make it valuable during times of transition. It imparts strength and grounding energy. Jasper is a stone of acceptance; this can mean accepting change and transcending limits. Jasper is associated with new beginnings and opportunities. Jasper can be used to increase self-esteem and emotional balance. It allows a person to see past disillusionment in order to make full use of their personal strengths. It can also be used to strengthen relationships, particularly long-term relationships.
- **Crystal History:** The history of jasper can be difficult to ascertain. While jasper is mentioned as one of the stones of power contained in the breastplate of the high priest in the book of Exodus, natural historians have not come to full agreement on whether the stone described was actually jasper. Its associations with strength and power have remained since ancient times. References to jasper occur in several different cultural texts dating back thousands of years.

Jet

◂ TUMBLED JET

- **Crystal Structure:** Amorphous
- **Focus:** Grounding, Protection, and Repelling
- **Color Range:** Black.
- **Characteristics:** Jet is technically not a crystal. A type of petrified wood, it is dense and glossy and hard enough to have the characteristics of a mineral, but not the regular crystal pattern that minerals must contain by definition. Jet is formed by the compression of wood and water and is actually a form of extremely dense coal. Jet is sometimes referred to as lignite. Its age is difficult to ascertain, as jet is truly prehistoric. It forms when mineral-bearing water comes into contact with wood.
- **Magickal Properties:** Jet is a powerful mineraloid frequently used in protection, grounding, and purification. It has the ability to aid in energetic cleansing and has even been attributed to healing damage to the aura. It is useful in apotropaic magick for warding off evil. Its protective abilities include warding off nightmares and dispelling fear.
- **Crystal History:** Because of its attractive black surface, jet has been traditionally used in a type of jewelry known as "memento mori," which is typically worn in remembrance of a person who has died. It has been used to comfort the bereaved and to dispel negative energy such as sorrow.

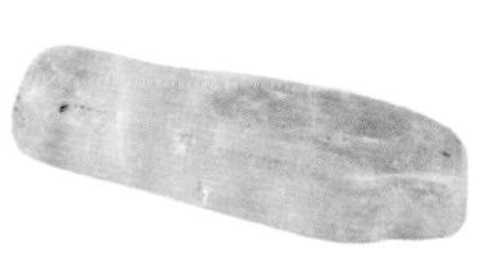

Kunzite

◀ TUMBLED KUNZITE CRYSTAL

- **CRYSTAL SYSTEM:** Monoclinic
- **FOCUS:** Heart Opening, Love, and Attraction
- **COLOR RANGE:** Violet and purple, pink, and, less commonly, green.
- **CHARACTERISTICS:** Kunzite is a relatively new crystal discovery that exhibits a phenomenon known as pleochroism, which is the ability to present different colors when viewed from different angles. Ranging from pale pink to deep violet, kunzite is one of the softer crystals and must be worn with care.
- **MAGICKAL PROPERTIES:** Kunzite has been described as a seductive stone. It is heavily associated with feminine energy and is useful in love magick, particularly in intensifying feelings of love. Kunzite is also used in manifestation magick; its attributes give it a power of attraction that allows you to call things to yourself. Kunzite has soothing properties that make it effective at dissipating anger.
- **CRYSTAL HISTORY:** Cataloged and named in 1902, kunzite references the American mineralogist George Frederick Kunz. Kunz was most famous for publishing an annual book on natal stones that was distributed to customers by the legendary New York jewelry company Tiffany & Co., which he was vice president of. Kunzite is considered one of his greatest contributions to the field of mineralogy.

Kyanite

ROUGH AND UNCUT KYANITE CRYSTALS

- **Crystal System:** Triclinic
- **Focus:** Restorer and Healer
- **Color Range:** Usually blue to indigo.
- **Characteristics:** Crystals of kyanite typically grow long and slender in bladelike formations with intense blue color. Some less valuable varieties will show flecks of gray or grayish blue or striated colors.
- **Magickal Properties:** Kyanite is a restorative crystal. Resonating with the heart, kyanite is used to restore emotional balance, enhance self-love, ward off negativity, and dispel distractions and confusion. Kyanite is believed to accelerate spiritual awakenings and promote astral travel. Owing to its restorative energy, kyanite can be used in dream work. It is an expansive stone: a heart opener as well as a dream awakener. Use kyanite when you need to be receptive to healing energy.
- **Crystal History:** Discovered in the late 1700s, kyanite is named for the Greek word for "blue," which is the most common color of these crystals; however, some specimens of orange kyanite have been found. Its color is reminiscent of the Aegean Sea, evoking a serene and dreamlike state.

Labradorite

CUT AND POLISHED LABRADORITE HEART

- **Crystal System:** Triclinic
- **Focus:** Revealer and Protector
- **Color Range:** Gray to dark gray with flashes of spectral colors.
- **Characteristics:** The unique iridescent flashes of color that labradorite exhibits have earned their own distinguishing term, "labradorescence." This effect is caused by different layers of the crystal structure working together to diffuse light. It is primarily found in Labrador, which it is named for, as well as in Finland and Madagascar. Varieties of labradorite that show intense labradorescence are called spectrolite.
- **Magickal Properties:** Labradorite is used magickally for many purposes, including prognosticating the future, protection for travelers, passion between lovers, and receiving psychic visions. It is often called a stone of adventure because of its exciting characteristics, particularly its display of multifaceted colors. It is used to improve relationships because its internal structure demands that different layers work together to produce colors that resonate with the throat, heart, and sacral chakras.
- **Crystal History:** Labradorite was first used by the Inuit, who referred to it as "fire stone." Powder made from labradorite was used as a medicinal remedy for physical ailments, and the stone itself was believed to have protective powers. It was collected in 1770 by a Morovian missionary in Canada and formally named in 1780 by Abraham Werner.

Lapis Lazuli

◀ TUMBLED LAPIS LAZULI WITH DISTINCT FLECKS OF METALLIC PYRITE

- **Crystal System:** None
- **Focus:** Awakener and Amplifier
- **Color Range:** Royal blue to dark blue with flecks of gold and white.
- **Characteristics:** Lapis lazuli does not have a crystal lattice structure, so by the scientific definition, lapis lazuli is not a crystal but a rock. It is composed of several different minerals, including lazurite, calcite, and pyrite, among others. It is primarily found in Afghanistan, Chile, and Russia. Lazurite gives lapis lazuli its deep blue violet color, while pyrite lends flecks of gold. Calcite presents as white streaks interspersed throughout the blue and gold.
- **Magickal Properties:** Due to its lengthy and rich history, intense blue color, and unique properties, lapis lazuli is a prized semiprecious gemstone. It has been used to open the third eye, strengthen bonds of friendship, elevate consciousness, and awaken its bearer to higher truths and greater power. Lapis lazuli also reveals past life connections and lessons. It can accelerate spiritual growth and reveals the lessons behind significant points of change.
- **Crystal History:** Lapis lazuli has a rich history and has been used by many cultures for close to ten thousand years. Lapis lazuli has adorned the gardens of ancient Babylon, accompanied Egyptian pharaohs into their tombs, and been used as pigment. When lapis lazuli is ground into a powder, this pigment is known as ultramarine.

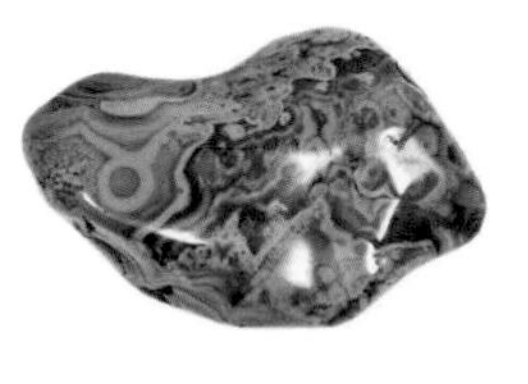

Malachite

◀ TUMBLED MALACHITE CRYSTAL

- **Crystal System:** Monoclinic
- **Focus:** Transformer and Revealer
- **Color Range:** Light to dark green with banded striation.
- **Characteristics:** Malachite is a stone of transformation, owing to its nature as a pseudomorph. Malachite can transform from cuprite, a red copper mineral. Its surface is glossy and smooth, but it can be easily damaged due to its relatively soft nature.
- **Magickal Properties:** Malachite is associated with transformation. It is a stone of enlightened leadership and can inspire confidence and creativity. Malachite increases the life force and has strong healing associations. Emotionally, malachite is a stone of clarity, while spiritually, it is used for psychic protection, manifestation, and empowering a witch's will. It is also used as a stone of abundance, increase, and success.
- **Crystal History:** Malachite is believed to have been mined and put to use around 4,000 B.C.E. It has been attributed to ancient Egypt and is sometimes called the "merchants' stone" due to its enduring desirability. It has also been associated with death and the afterlife, but also wealth.

Moonstone

TUMBLED MOONSTONE CRYSTAL

- **CRYSTAL SYSTEM:** Monoclinic
- **FOCUS:** Clairvoyance, Feminine Power, and Receiver
- **COLOR RANGE:** Clear, white, blue, and peach.
- **CHARACTERISTICS:** Moonstone is a feldspar crystal and as such is one of the most common mineral groups on the planet. Because moonstone crystallizes with alternating layers of albite and orthoclase, a spectacular effect called schiller occurs. Moonstone possesses the best example of this effect. In a quality moonstone crystal, you will see a hovering light that appears to emanate from within the crystal as well as float above it. This optical property of a glowing light moving across the surface of the crystal is also known as adularescence. Moonstone will exhibit adularescence in any color.
- **MAGICKAL PROPERTIES:** Moonstone can activate your intuition, which is deeply connected to psychic abilities such as clairvoyance. Symbolic of feminine power, moonstone can be helpful in drawing power and in meditation. Moonstone is a powerful aid to manifestation magick and channeling. The schiller effect creates a cone of light with the apex emanating from the stone and the base projecting outward to the universe like a receiving vessel of light.
- **CRYSTAL HISTORY:** Believed to be influenced by the phases of the moon, moonstone was named by Pliny the Elder and admired throughout ancient Greece and Rome. In northern Europe, moonstone is considered a birthstone for the month of June. Popular in ancient Greece and Rome, the Renaissance, and the Art Nouveau period, the allure of moonstone persists to this day.

Obsidian

◀ ROUGH AND UNCUT BROWN OBSIDIAN

- **Crystal System:** Amorphous
- **Focus:** Strength, Grounding, and Protection
- **Color Range:** Glossy dark black or black, brown, or gray with white spots or flecks.
- **Characteristics:** Obsidian is actually a type of glass that forms when lava cools rapidly, causing the formation of what appears to be short crystals. Because obsidian is an igneous rock and has no crystal lattice structure, it is considered a mineraloid (and it strongly resembles a crystal). Brown obsidian is sometimes referred to as Apache Tears.
- **Magickal Properties:** Obsidian is a perfect stone to reach for in times of need. It is both grounding and protective and eliminates energy blockages. If you are seeking to invigorate your intentions and bring new life to your endeavors, obsidian is an excellent strengthening tool. Obsidian is also helpful in guarding against self-sabotage. It offers protection against negative self-talk and judgment and is known to enhance communication with the spirit realm. Obsidian can help strengthen perseverance and provide insight, particularly about past lives.
- **Crystal History:** Though obsidian has been known for over nine thousand years, its origins are not entirely clear. Some say it was discovered in Mesopotamia, while others claim it was discovered by a Roman explorer named either Obsius or Obsidius who found the glassy mineral-like substance in Ethiopia. Another theory is that obsidian was named for the Greek word "obsis," meaning "spectacle," because it was used as a mirror.

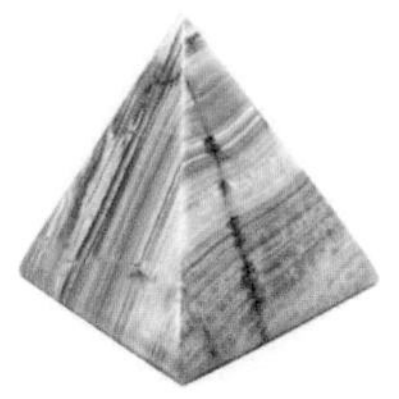

Onyx

◀ CUT AND POLISHED MULTICOLORED BANDED ONYX PYRAMID

- **Crystal System:** Trigonal with individual units that can only be seen with magnification
- **Focus:** Releasing and Banishing
- **Color Range:** Black, brown, red, and green.
- **Characteristics:** Onyx is a type of agate that is either all one color or shows some bands of contrasting colors. It has a waxy luster and occurs in a variety of colors, the most well-known of which is black. It is used in magick, as a decorative crystal in carvings such as cameos, and in jewelry. When onyx is red, it is referred to as sardonyx.
- **Magickal Properties:** Strongly associated with separation, onyx is a powerful crystal to use when releasing things that no longer serve you. Onyx has a calming energy, making it extremely useful during times of transition, breakups, and other endings of relationships. Onyx can remove unwanted energy and dispel negativity, and it is particularly helpful when you find yourself needing to reverse course or redirect your energy. Onyx is a stone of discipline and can help develop willpower and increase inner strength.
- **Crystal History:** In 1560, the Italian Renaissance mathematician Girolamo Cardano described onyx as having an ability to quell passion between lovers, leading to its modern association with separation. In parts of Asia such as India and China, black onyx was considered unlucky and was used primarily for trade, but in Myanmar, statues were carved from onyx and kept in the home. Known for thousands of years, onyx is a crystal that has attracted spiritual energy as well as superstition.

Opal

◀ ROUGH AND UNCUT OPAL

- **CRYSTAL SYSTEM:** Amorphous
- **FOCUS:** Protection and Receiving
- **COLOR RANGE:** White or clear with flashes of spectral colors.
- **CHARACTERISTICS:** A soft variety of quartz, opal gets its unique flashes of spectral colors from water droplets trapped within layers of the mineral. This visually appealing display of color is known as opalescence. It can present as intense flashes of blue, green, pink, orange, and red. Opal is also a pseudomorph that can take on the crystal structure of other minerals although it does not have a regular lattice pattern of its own. It is found in Australia, the United States, and Mexico.
- **MAGICKAL PROPERTIES:** Opal is associated with channeling and receiving messages. It is considered a stone of hope that can increase a witch's ability to access intuition, making it useful for expanding consciousness and amplifying creativity. Opal is also used in protective magick and in dream interpretation as well as to encourage or inhibit certain types of dreams. Although it is a fragile crystal, it is also spiritually powerful and should be handled with care.
- **CRYSTAL HISTORY:** Opal was known to be valued by ancient Romans and is believed to have been discovered first in Africa. Opal has been described as the happy tears of the god Zeus in ancient Greece, while in the Middle East, it was believed to have fallen from the sky. Modern superstition holds that opal is unlucky when given as a gift, most likely due to its soft nature.

Peridot

◀ ROUGH AND UNCUT PERIDOT CRYSTAL

- **Crystal System:** Orthorhombic
- **Focus:** Relationship Healer
- **Color Range:** Light green to olive green.
- **Characteristics:** Peridot is a type of olivine in that when olivine is especially transparent and vivid, it is classified as peridot. While olivine is one of the most widely occurring minerals in the entire solar system, peridot is much rarer. Peridot has cleavage planes in two directions, which can make it susceptible to breakage.
- **Magickal Properties:** Peridot is useful in promoting harmony in significant love relationships such as marriage and domestic partnerships. Heart opening and soothing, peridot is believed to bring people closer together and can be useful in healing emotional upset or restoring equilibrium in relationships that have fallen out of balance.
- **Crystal History:** Dozens of miles from the shores of Egypt was the first known origin of peridot. For more than two thousand years, the island of Zabargad produced these gems that captivated early Greeks and Romans, as well as dynasties from Egypt and Arabia, as is evidenced by ancient texts. Some scholars believe that some of Cleopatra's famed emeralds might actually have been peridot.

Prasiolite

◀ ROUGH AND UNCUT PRASIOLITE CRYSTAL

- **Crystal System:** Trigonal
- **Focus:** Renewal and Growth
- **Color Range:** Light green to olivine green.
- **Characteristics:** Prasiolite is a transparent variety of quartz that gets its green color from trace amounts of iron embedded in the crystal lattice. It is sometimes identified by the misnomer "green amethyst" because the green color can also be produced through heat treatment, and in some cases, exposure to radiation. The seafoam green color of prasiolite is somewhat delicate. Prasiolite can fade if it is exposed to too much heat.
- **Magickal Properties:** Prasiolite represents divine love and compassion. Prasiolite crystals can put you in touch with your higher self. They are wonderful tools for personal growth and invoking new situations. Prasiolite can keep you centered when you are navigating a change of environment. Like the unfurling of the first leaves of spring, the light green color and transparent nature of prasiolite encourages you to be open to new experiences and to be able to discern the places where you need to be focusing your energy in order to serve your higher purpose.
- **Crystal History:** Prasiolite was discovered in eastern Europe in the early 1800s. Natural deposits have been recorded in Poland, Brazil, and parts of California. Its name references a vegetable, as it is derived from the Greek word "práso" which means "leek." A relatively new crystal discovery, prasiolite deposits often occur together with amethyst and citrine, as they are all quartz group crystals.

Pyrite

NATURAL PYRITE CLUSTER

- **CRYSTAL SYSTEM:** Cubic
- **FOCUS:** Prosperity, Abundance, and Wealth
- **COLOR RANGE:** Metallic gold.
- **CHARACTERISTICS:** Pyrite is easy to recognize due to its bright metallic luster. Pyrite is relatively hard and is often found together with other elements such as gold, silver, and copper.
- **MAGICKAL PROPERTIES:** Pyrite is a crystal of action. Due to its metallic luster, it is strongly associated with wealth and prosperity. Frequently used in money drawing spells, pyrite is also helpful as a ward against negativity. Pyrite crystals can bolster your ability to make strong and bold choices, and it is useful in shadow work, particularly work involving overcoming fears. Associated with masculine energy, pyrite carries with it the energy signature of confidence, vitality, creativity, and vitality. It can also strengthen your willpower.
- **CRYSTAL HISTORY:** The name "pyrite" is a derivative of "pyr," meaning "fire" in Greek. In addition to its metallic color, pyrite is also associated with fire due to the fact that it can emit sparks when struck by another, harder mineral. For this reason, pyrite was used in early European flintlocks. In the California gold rush of the 1800s, pyrite was often confused with gold by prospectors, leading it to be called "fool's gold."

Quartz (Clear)

CUT AND POLISHED CLEAR QUARTZ TOWER (L) WITH NATURAL CLEAR QUARTZ CLUSTER (R)

- **CRYSTAL SYSTEM:** Trigonal
- **FOCUS:** Clarity, Amplifier, Conductor, and Omniscience
- **COLOR RANGE:** Clear and transparent with white inclusions.
- **CHARACTERISTICS:** One of the most abundant minerals on earth, quartz is found everywhere from mountaintops to beaches. It is a truly omnipresent crystal with metaphysical, technological, decorative, and architectural applications. Quartz forms in clusters of six-sided prisms and has piezoelectric qualities, which means it can generate electricity when heat and pressure are applied to it.
- **MAGICKAL PROPERTIES:** Because it is so common and so very useful, quartz is a magickally powerful crystal. It is used as an aid in meditation, to direct intentions, to store and transfer energy, and to heal spiritual and emotional wounds. Quartz is uplifting, improves concentration, and can help provide clarity in divinations. Quartz can align the spirit with higher realms and raise your energy vibration.
- **CRYSTAL HISTORY:** Quartz is one of the most ancient magick crystals, with a history dating back nearly seven thousand years to the earliest civilizations of Mesopotamia. Upon its first discovery in ancient Greece, quartz was believed to be enchanted ice that would never melt.

Rhodochrosite

RHODOCHROSITE TUMBLED CRYSTAL

- **Crystal System:** Trigonal
- **Focus:** Healing and Attraction
- **Color Range:** Rhodochrosite presents in rose, pink, and red tones and is characterized by striations of color.
- **Characteristics:** Rhodochrosite is a very distinct crystal and is easily recognizable due to its rosy pink to red colors and consistent bands. When scratched on a hard surface, rhodochrosite will leave a white streak. Some of the finest-quality rhodochrosite comes from Argentina.
- **Magickal Properties:** Rhodochrosite is a powerful healing crystal, particularly in matters of the heart. It is considered a protective stone and is associated with goddess energy. Rhodochrosite can inspire forgiveness and has been called the "rescue remedy" of crystals (a reference to the Bach Original Flower Remedies). It can also be used in protective magick, as it has associations with the Devi of India. Think of rhodochrosite as a protective mother, able to forgive, to heal, and to manifest while reducing anxiety and stress. It can encourage you to have a positive outlook, soothe emotional upsets, and energize your soul.
- **Crystal History:** Discovered in 1813 in Romania, rhodochrosite was used in ornamental carvings and in jewelry and remains a sought-after crystal today. The deposits in Catamarca, Argentina, are the most significant source of rhodochrosite. Around 10,000 pounds of rhodochrosite exhibiting concentric patterns of color were found growing in stalactites and stalagmites in a thirteenth-century Inca silver mine.

Rose Quartz

ROUGH AND UNCUT ROSE QUARTZ CRYSTAL

- **Crystal System:** Trigonal
- **Focus:** Expansive Love
- **Color Range:** Pale pink.
- **Characteristics:** Because threads of another silicate mineral are woven through the crystal lattice, rose quartz often has a very hazy appearance. It is very rare to see a transparent or clear rose quartz crystal. Sometimes the internal fibers align to produce a star effect known as an asterism. Rose quartz is found mainly in Brazil, India, and Madagascar. It almost always grows in massive crystals.
- **Magickal Properties:** There is perhaps no other crystal that is more synonymous with love than rose quartz. Rose quartz can open you to all types of love: platonic, romantic, familial, and self-love. Rose quartz elevates and inspires emotional intimacy and trust. It encourages affection, balances emotional states, eases disappointments, and dissipates anger.
- **Crystal History:** Rose quartz has an illustrious and ancient history dating back as long as seven thousand years ago. It is believed to have first been used by Assyrians to fashion beads. Romans used rose quartz in seals to signify ownership, while Egyptians believed that rose quartz would preserve youth.

Ruby

◀ ROUGH AND UNCUT RUBY CRYSTAL

- **CRYSTAL SYSTEM:** Trigonal
- **FOCUS:** Vitality and Passion
- **COLOR RANGE:** Ruby is the red variety of corundum and is only ever shades of red. If the color of corundum varies into pink, the stone is no longer considered a ruby. Ruby red has been described as the color of blood, and the most valuable rubies are referred to as "pigeon's blood."
- **CHARACTERISTICS:** Ruby is a very hard stone and is often used as an abrasive due to its resistance to scratching. It is found in metamorphic limestone that has been worn away by erosion. It is also found in river streams and lakes, most notably in a 25-square-mile area in Myanmar. Ruby has also been found in Cambodia, Thailand, India, Switzerland, and Tanzania.
- **MAGICKAL PROPERTIES:** Ruby is said to represent the life force. It is a highly prized stone of passion and strength. Ruby can inspire courage, promote an adventurous spirit, and increase enthusiasm. Ruby is used in love magick in order to amplify and intensify ardor. It can also sharpen the mind's focus, particularly when concentration is needed on a singular task. Life, energy, and strength of spirit are all associated with ruby. It is also used for protection.
- **CRYSTAL HISTORY:** Ruby has been mined for thousands of years. In ancient China, ruby was incorporated into armor for certain nobles, as it was believed to carry protective powers. In the mid-twentieth century, ruby was used in the development of lasers. Primarily found in Myanmar, formerly known as Burma, ruby is a rare gem, and due to its scarcity, it is often imitated. Ancient Romans were known to incorporate imitation ruby in their adornments.

Sapphire

ROUGH AND UNCUT BLUE SAPPHIRE CRYSTAL

- **CRYSTAL SYSTEM:** Trigonal
- **FOCUS:** Clarity and Calming
- **COLOR RANGE:** Sapphire occurs in a multitude of colors from purple and mauve to green and blue, even yellow, orange, and pink, almost every color except for red.
- **CHARACTERISTICS:** Sapphire is a precious gemstone due to its transparency, hardness, and relative rarity. It is prized for its durability and color. Sapphire is found in many places, including Sri Lanka, Madagascar, Australia, India, Columbia, and the United States, primarily Montana.
- **MAGICKAL PROPERTIES:** Sapphire is used to communicate with the spiritual realm. It is a crystal of clarity and is associated with loyalty, making it useful in magick centered on or around relationships. Peaceful and calming, sapphire has a positive effect on the mind and can aid in the development of psychic abilities. It is often associated with feminine power.
- **CRYSTAL HISTORY:** Historically, uses of sapphire have been spiritual in nature throughout the world. Because it frequently occurs in shades of blue, sapphire was believed to be connected to heaven. It was worn in ancient Greece when oracles were consulted. It has been used as a tool for augmenting spiritual connections by Buddhists and Hindus.

Selenite

◀ TUMBLED SELENITE CRYSTAL

- **Crystal System:** Monoclinic
- **Focus:** Clarity and Clairvoyance
- **Color Range:** Selenite can appear clear, yellow, or white with adularescence.
- **Characteristics:** Selenite crystals will sometimes become embedded with sand and water during formation, which results in a "rose" formation, sometimes referred to as a desert rose or a selenite rose.
- **Magickal Properties:** Selenite is very useful for aiding the decision-making process. It can bring about a deep state of calm and peace. Selenite is considered an "angel stone" because it can be used to simultaneously guide and shield those who use it for magick. When selenite presents in its "rose" form, it is used to reveal inner truths, enhance mental clarity, and bring one into an increased state of awareness of both the environment and the self.
- **Crystal History:** Selenite was named for the moon, no doubt owing to its glowing sheen caused by the play of light among layers of gypsum, which strongly resembles the effect of sunlight reflecting off of the surface of the moon. It was first described in 1747 by the Swedish mineralogist J.G. Wallerius.

Smoky Quartz

◀ CUT AND POLISHED SMOKY QUARTZ TOWER

- **Crystal System:** Trigonal
- **Focus:** Protection, Grounding, and Growth
- **Color Range:** Light brown to dark golden brown, smoky gray to black.
- **Characteristics:** Trace amounts of aluminum and natural radiation give smoky quartz its distinctive color. It is found in Scotland, Brazil, Madagascar, and Australia.
- **Magickal Properties:** Smoky quartz has a unique ability to help you attune to nature. It heals the etheric body and can help you develop your psychic gifts. It is extremely grounding and can transmute energy. Smoky quartz is especially useful for deflecting and dissipating negative energy. It can also inspire creativity, increase happiness, and accelerate spiritual growth. Smoky quartz is a stone of great power.
- **Crystal History:** Hundreds of years ago in China, smoky quartz was used in what could probably be considered the first sunglasses. During the Victorian era, smoky quartz was often used in mourning jewelry. It is also the official crystal of Scotland.

Sodalite

◀ TUMBLED SODALITE CRYSTAL

- **Crystal System:** Cubic
- **Focus:** Psychic Abilities, Communication, and Strength
- **Color Range:** Light to dark royal blue with white veining.
- **Characteristics:** Sodalite forms when high-sodium magma crystalizes. It doesn't contain many silicate minerals or even aluminum, so while it resembles feldspar, it chemically is not. It can range from light to dark blue and usually has distinct streaks of white calcite veins throughout.
- **Magickal Properties:** Sodalite allows you to access your subconscious mind. If you are interested in developing your intuitive abilities, sodalite is an excellent crystal to work with. It can enhance mental clarity, allowing you to access new depths of awareness that combine intuition and acuity. Sodalite has protective powers when you find yourself needing to speak up in situations where there is a power differential. It is useful in improving communication and giving you the strength to make your voice heard. Sodalite is a rational crystal that invites objectivity and clear thinking.
- **Crystal History:** Sodalite was discovered in Greenland in the early 1800s and was possibly used much earlier as a trading commodity in parts of South America. Because of its rare blue color, it is used in ornamental carvings and in jewelry.

Sunstone

◀ TUMBLED SUNSTONE CRYSTAL

- **CRYSTAL SYSTEM:** Triclinic
- **FOCUS:** Good Fortune and Positivity
- **COLOR RANGE:** Peach, orange, and brown with flecks of copper.
- **CHARACTERISTICS:** Sunstone may contain copper inclusions or even hematite inclusions that create the aventurescence schiller effect. Sunstone often appears as though it has sparkling lights interspersed throughout its lattice. Sunstone is also a type of labradorite. It is found in northern Europe, Australia, India, Mexico, and the United States, with Oregon being a particularly notable source.
- **MAGICKAL PROPERTIES:** Sunstone is an auspicious crystal that is known to bring good luck. It can increase vitality and amplify positive energy. It can help bolster your convictions and boost confidence, making it extremely useful during those times you need the assistance of others in order to move your life forward.
- **CRYSTAL HISTORY:** Sunstone has a rich magickal history across diverse cultures. Indigenous American lore holds that the crystal was formed from drops of blood shed by a great warrior who was wounded by an enemy arrow. His spirit then entered the crystal, giving it supernatural power. Sunstone is also associated with Viking lore. Early navigators would hold sunstone up against a cloudy sky in order to determine the location of the sun.

Tiger's Eye

◀ TUMBLED TIGER'S EYE CRYSTAL

- **Crystal System:** Trigonal
- **Focus:** Courage, Protection, and Strength
- **Color Range:** Golden brown to yellow.
- **Characteristics:** Tiger's eye is a particularly distinct type of quartz crystal, noted for its chatoyancy. This effect is caused by alternating layers of quartz crystals growing with a different type of mineral called amphibole. The result is a glowing line of light effect that mimics the appearance of a feline eye.
- **Magickal Properties:** In addition to being a protective stone, tiger's eye is also used for recuperation and purification. It is associated with strengthening psychic sight and bolstering courage. Tiger's eye is useful when navigating difficult situations. It can protect you from psychic attacks and empower you to confront uncomfortable situations. The cat's eye effect exhibited by tiger's eye gives it correspondences to the sun, which explains why it has been used to revive low energy, particularly after overindulgences.
- **Crystal History:** Tiger's eye was originally categorized in 1784 by the French scientist François Levaillant, but its use is believed to date back to ancient Egypt, where it was used in protective amulets. Tiger's eye was believed to contain the rays of the sun, and for this reason, regenerative powers were associated with it.

Topaz

ROUGH AND UNCUT WHITE TOPAZ WITH GOLDEN TOPAZ

- **Crystal System:** Orthorhombic
- **Focus:** Psychic Abilities, Manifestation, and Strength
- **Color Range:** Topaz occurs naturally in white, yellow, red, orange, brown, green, and blue; however, the fantastic mystical colors and electric blue that topaz is known for is caused by irradiation and coatings; these are not naturally occurring effects. Yellow topaz can turn pink when it is heated. The golden variety is the most precious and rare and is referred to as imperial topaz.
- **Characteristics:** Topaz has prismatic faces that show striations in color. Its strong cleavage allows it to break cleanly. Topaz is one of the rarer silicate crystals, and it can be very expensive in natural and transparent colors. Topaz is found throughout the world, including Brazil, Madagascar, China, Russia, Namibia, Mexico, and Pakistan.
- **Magickal Properties:** Topaz is used for seeing beyond and for calling desires and dreams from the plane of the subconscious into reality. Topaz has been used psychically for contacting spirits and opening channels of communication beyond the veil. It can elevate your energy, making metaphysical realms approachable. Beautiful and empowering, topaz's metaphysical properties are wide, mainly due to the many colors in which it naturally occurs.
- **Crystal History:** Ancient Egyptians believed that topaz was imbued with mystical powers granted by the sun and that it could make its bearer invisible. Because of its rarity, it was believed to occur only on an island in the Red Sea that in ancient times was called Topazios, from the word "topazein," meaning "to seek" or "to conjecture," owing to topaz's elusive nature.

Tourmaline

TUMBLED WATERMELON TOURMALINE CRYSTAL

- **Crystal System:** Trigonal
- **Focus:** Protection and Success
- **Color Range:** Tourmaline comes in all colors of the rainbow from pink to green, watermelon, dark pink, and even black. It is highly sought-after and very popular due to its wide range of beautiful colors.
- **Characteristics:** Tourmaline describes a wide group of boron silicate minerals that all share the same crystal structure but have different chemical compositions that show up in the array of colors in which tourmaline occurs. It is a hydrothermal crystal, formed when heated water carries the necessary elements into a pocket in the earth. Tourmaline is a durable crystal and can survive being carried down a river.
- **Magickal Properties:** Magickal uses of tourmaline vary depending on its color. For example, black tourmaline is very effective for use in protective magick, grounding, and cleansing, while green tourmaline is used for spells invoking prosperity, success, and growth. Rubellite tourmaline is better suited for matters of the heart. Other uses of tourmaline include balancing the emotions, enlightenment, and business success.
- **Crystal History:** The history of tourmaline dates back approximately five hundred years when it was accidentally discovered as a by-product of alluvial gold mining. Portuguese explorers brought tourmaline from Brazil, believing it to be emerald and ruby. In the 1800s, tourmaline was discovered in the United States in Maine.

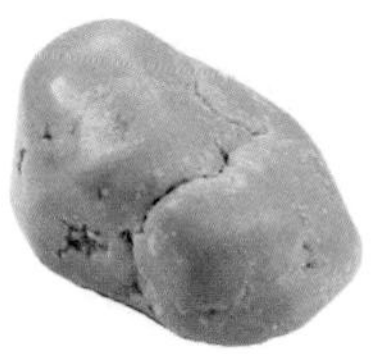

Turquoise

ROUGH AND UNCUT TURQUOISE CRYSTAL

- **Crystal System:** Triclinic
- **Focus:** Expansion and Communication
- **Color Range:** Light to medium greenish blue.
- **Characteristics:** Turquoise is opaque, but lends itself to carving, making it one of the ornamental gems. It is relatively soft and occurs mainly in very dry regions of the world, with some of the most beautiful turquoise crystals coming from Iran. It is prominently used in Indigenous American carvings and jewelry. Turquoise will often contain veins of its host matrix running through it.
- **Magickal Properties:** Turquoise is a stone of spiritual expansion, but it is also used to inspire forgiveness and to cultivate a positive self-image. Turquoise improves communication and is a healing crystal. It inspires compassion and can help you face difficult truths.
- **Crystal History:** Nearly one and a half million years ago, turquoise was discovered in the American northwest. In New Mexico, Indigenous people mined an entire mountain, reducing Mount Chalchihuitl to a pit. Traditional use of turquoise among many tribes such as Navajo, Hopi, Zuni, and Kewa included ritual offerings, beautification, and trade.

Unakite

◀ TUMBLED UNAKITE CRYSTAL

- **CRYSTAL SYSTEM:** Monoclinic
- **FOCUS:** Road Opener and Psychic Awareness
- **COLOR RANGE:** Both earthy and rosy, unakite is most often seen as mossy or olivine green with flecks of pink, red, and brown.
- **CHARACTERISTICS:** Unakite is composed of several minerals, including epidote, quartz, and orthoclase. Part of the feldspar group, it is sometimes described as a "sister" to moonstone because the two crystals share a family and aspects of their composition. Unakite is a remarkably versatile crystal and has been used in everything from jewelry to architecture, tiles, and even road construction.
- **MAGICKAL PROPERTIES:** Unakite helps a witch deal with blockages. It is a remover of obstacles and is particularly useful for spells that involve growth and rebirth. Unakite is a centering crystal. It helps maintain focus in the present moment and aligns the consciousness in the necessary interaction between thinking and doing. Unakite represents the unity of thought and action. Unakite is often associated with clairvoyance because it is referred to as a stone of vision.
- **CRYSTAL HISTORY:** Discovered in North Carolina and named for the Unaka Mountains, unakite was first described in the 1870s. A type of granite, unakite has been put to myriad uses. In addition to North Carolina and Tennessee, unakite has also been discovered in South Africa and Brazil, as well as Russia and China.

Wulfenite

NATURAL WULFENITE CRYSTAL CLUSTER

- **Crystal System:** Tetragonal
- **Focus:** Connection and Heightened Sensitivity
- **Color Range:** Wulfenite is most often seen in colors ranging from light yellow to a fiery red, but it also presents as orange together with olive green.
- **Characteristics:** It often forms in thin, tabular crystals with brown inclusions. Soft and fragile, wulfenite is sought-after for its color. It is rare to see cut and polished wulfenite crystals. Wulfenite has been found in Algeria, Congo, Morocco, the Czech Republic, Slovakia, Queensland, Australia, Mexico, and Arizona.
- **Magickal Properties:** Wulfenite is used as a bridge to connect the lower chakras. It is also used for restoring energy, enhancing creativity, and spiritual growth. Enlivening and stimulating, wulfenite can attune a witch to sensitive vibrations. Wulfenite allows you to access your vulnerable side without being subjected to harm.
- **Crystal History:** Named for Franz Xaver von Wulfen, an eighteenth-century mineralogist, wulfenite was discovered during a search for lead ore. It was less frequently referred to as melinose due to its rich amber color, as "meli" is associated with the Greek word for "honey."

PART THREE

HOW TO USE CRYSTALS IN MAGICK

Now that you have a foundation in the magickal principles that direct crystal magick, it is within your power to apply these laws to your own spells. Using crystals can help you with everything from amplifying your fortune, to your relationships, and even your appearance. With numerous spells and rituals from simple to complex, the following chapters will give you specific activities that incorporate crystals according to the systems of magick that govern how you interact with them as a witch. You will develop and hone your powers of magick by using crystals in many different capacities, all with the intention to improve your success in whatever aspect of life you need to give attention to.

Chapter 4

CRYSTALS for LUCK and PROSPERITY

Crystals can teach you valuable lessons about prosperity by their existence alone. Any crystal can be considered a token of luck because it takes a good deal of luck for any geologist, mineral collector, or rock hound to locate a crystal-bearing pocket and unearth its contents without causing a lot of damage. And while every crystal will have some kind of auspicious luck connected to it by nature of its discovery, some crystals are better suited for abundance magick than others.

Spells for abundance can incorporate crystals in many ways. In this chapter, you will learn about which crystals to use for drawing abundance, money, luck, and prosperity, along with different crystal lattice and matrix configurations that will aid your focus in manifesting what you seek.

USING CRYSTALS FOR ABUNDANCE

The concept of prosperity is relatively straightforward: You are able to meet your basic needs in such a way that they flow toward you unhindered by obstacles. Scarcity and lack is replaced with abundance and prosperity. You are doing more than just surviving. You are thriving! If you feel that you are stuck in survival mode due to a lack of abundance, crystals can help you refocus your energy where it needs to be in order to attain the receptive mental state that will allow you to take inventory of your advantages and work them to their fullest potential.

All spells focused on prosperity and abundance must be accompanied by an alignment of action on your part. You cannot do a spell to banish debt and continue to live beyond your means. Using crystal magick to increase your means allows you to shift your mindset and make mental room for the level of abundance that you seek. Abundance is having enough for yourself with a surplus that can be shared. By enacting spells of abundance, you are using imitative magick, and by aligning your deeds with your intentions, you are acting in accord. These are powerful magickal principles used by modern witches across the globe.

These are the crystals used most often in spells for luck and prosperity:

- Amber
- Aventurine
- Citrine
- Green fluorite
- Heliodor
- Jade
- Malachite
- Peridot
- Prasiolite
- Pyrite
- Sunstone
- Topaz
- Tourmaline

MONEY DRAWING SPELL FOR INCREASING ABUNDANCE

Scarcity is something that needs to be counteracted, and using crystals and magick is an empowering way to confront what for many is a fraught issue. Your relationship to money is complex. Developing healthy attitudes toward money is important, and incorporating crystals into spells of abundance infuses growth intentions with positive vibrations.

Money Drawing Spell for Increasing Abundance

You Will Need

- 10 small tumbled crystals (a mix of aventurine, malachite, prasiolite)
- Stick of incense
- Incense holder
- Compass
- Green candle
- Cup of water
- Double-terminated quartz crystal, as clear as possible
- Index card or small square of special paper
- Pen
- Paper currency, at least 3 bills of the highest denomination available to you
- Grimoire, journal, or notebook

Directions

1. Prepare your altar by clearing and cleaning it. This means removing and storing any objects, effigies, or tools that you have been previously working with. You will need a fresh start and a "blank slate" for this spell. This also gives you a chance to take stock of what you already have. As you remove each object, treat it with care as though it is very valuable. Thank the object for its magickal presence in your craft and focus on what you have. It doesn't have to be formal, but it does have to be true and it does need to be spoken aloud. It can be as simple as "I give thanks for this candle. My life is warm and bright. I have a lot of candles because I can easily afford them." Or "I give thanks for this incense burner because it was a gift from a friend. My relationships are strong and I am greatly loved." Or "I give thanks for this miniature cauldron that I bought myself because I am an actualized person and I am worthy of respect. I can make decisions for myself and my decisions are correct for me." Continue in this manner until your altar is clear. Remove any dust and debris. For an energy bonus, you can use crystal-infused water to do a simple cleansing by moistening a paper towel or a washcloth and wiping down your surfaces.
2. Once you have cleared your space, take a few moments to focus on yourself and the work at hand. Hold your crystals as you formulate a clear and specific need in your mind. Put the crystals down and start the spell by first lighting the stick of incense (this will also be your measure of time). Place the incense in the holder and put it on your altar, preferably in the corner or area that most closely aligns with the east.

Use a compass to determine which areas of your altar are most closely aligned with the compass rose. Call upon the powers to assist you:

I invoke the spirits of air that favorable winds may bring seeds to soil.

3. Light the green candle and put it in the southernmost area; say:

   I invoke the spirits of fire that as the light grows, so do my fortunes.

4. Place the cup of water on the altar across from the incense; say:

   I invoke the spirits of water, that abundance and prosperity flow freely to me.

5. Place the double-terminated quartz crystal vertically with one of the points pointing toward the center of your altar. And say:

   I invoke the spirits of the earth, as I receive her bounty and riches.

6. Now take the index card or slip of paper and write down only the number (*without any currency symbol*) representing the amount of money that you need. Next, write a "1" to the left of the number and a "0" to the right. Then add the currency symbol.
7. Place the card faceup in the center of your altar and cover it with the paper money. One by one, place the tumbled stones on top of the currency. As you place each stone, envision the number increasing from the number you originally wrote to the final number after you added the one and the zero. Recite the following charm to create the spell:

   Cross my palm with silver
   Cross my palm with gold
   Money more than meets my needs
   More than I can hold
   Enough for me to meet my dreams
   Enough to meet my ends
   Enough to fill my bank accounts
   Enough to share with friends.

8. Hold your hands over the crystals as you envision money flowing into your hands. When this vision is clear, take out your grimoire and begin to break down the tasks at hand. You have ten stones in front of you. You will dedicate each to a specific purpose, and touch each stone as you write down its purpose. Some examples are:

- Ten ways to make ten dollars
- Ten ways to make a hundred dollars
- Ten ways to make a thousand dollars

9. When you come up with your list, it should be very specific to your abilities. Pick up a crystal one at a time and speak its purpose, holding it in front of your lips. Place it back on top of the currency until all ten crystals are imbued with the sound vibration of the purpose that you have spoken aloud.
10. Check on your incense stick. If it has not gone out, continue to focus on your spoken and written endeavors. Then choose one to begin with. Pick the crystal that coincides with your first endeavor and carry it around with you in the same pocket or wallet or purse where you keep your money. Keep it as a reminder of what you have invoked. Every time you touch it, you put yourself in alignment with your goal of increasing your money. When the first action is complete, replace the crystal on your altar and pick up the next one. If you find that one idea is taking off, stick with it. Enjoy finding new ways to create money and accept the prosperity that rightly flows to you.

SUMMONING ABUNDANCE AND CONJURING CASH

If you are in need of receiving a small amount of money in a short time frame, you can build a quick crystal charm for your altar.

Magick Current Money Drawing Spell

You Will Need

- Small slip of paper (about half the size of the paper currency)
- Pen
- Paper currency such as one dollar bill, pound note, or euro in any denomination, the higher the amount, the better
- Double-terminated crystal point
- 18 inches of metallic gold thread

Directions

1. On the slip of paper, write down the dollar amount that you need.
2. Place the slip of paper on top of the currency. Fold the currency lengthwise over the paper in thirds. The paper will no longer be visible.
3. Wrap the currency around the crystal point and secure it with the thread. Touch one point of the crystal and name it as the source the money will come from. Some examples are through luck, through chance, through work, through generosity, through kindness, and so on.
4. Touch the other point of the crystal and name it as the destination where the money will arrive. For example, your wallet, your purse, your pocket, your bank account, by direct deposit, and so on.
5. Now hold the charm between your palms and blow on it as you visualize the source and destination. When the vision is clear, place the charm on your altar and seal the spell with a specific chant such as:

   By luck, by fate, by three times three
   The money I need will come to me.

   Or

   By work and skill, my endeavors succeed
   And I will get the money I need.

   Or

   All those that have
   My need they will see
   And that which I seek
   Will be given to me.

6. Finally, be on the lookout for small amounts of money turning up in unexpected places through either gifts, forgotten places, or new opportunities. Keep the crystal in a prominent place as a reminder to keep yourself in a receptive mindset. Accept money when it is offered.

CRYSTAL SPELL OF INCREASE

Perhaps you already have money and you need it to grow, or you have successfully banished your debt with magickal assistance and now you need a substantial loan. If your endeavors are taking off, you can use crystal magick to amplify your increase.

Crystal Spell of Increase

You Will Need

- Paper currency or check stubs or copies of checks that you have received from other people, the higher the amount, the better. Use 3 or more bills: 1 for the charger and the others to surround it.
- Metal charger or plate, such as a brass or silver plate
- Crystal tower, pillar, or obelisk
- Lots of coins in varying denominations

Directions

1. Take the highest denomination of paper currency and place it on the charger. Place the crystal on top of the currency on the charger.
2. Surround the base of the crystal with coins so it looks abundant, with some coins stacked and others in small layered piles.
3. Fold any remaining currency and tuck it in between the crystal and the coins. This is a crucial step because it is difficult. During this part of the spell you will be called to examine how your handle money. You will have to be careful, decisive, and anticipate disruptions or actions that upset the balance. Give yourself a pep talk by repeating affirmations such as "I handle money with skill" or "I am capable of difficult things" or "I meet challenges with creativity." You don't want to be careless or messy with this step by sending coins rolling away from your crystal. It's not supposed to be easy. It's supposed to help you cultivate intention and attention to action and consequence.
4. Touch the point of the crystal with the index finger of your dominant hand. Close your eyes and envision a firehose of money pouring in through the window of your home or business. Repeat over and over:

   Money flows, money grows, money pays, money stays.

5. Do this as often as necessary when you feel any thoughts of scarcity or need creeping in on your magickal radiant power. Keep the items on your altar for as long as you need. Remember that you can also place additional crystals, coins, and currency on the altar to keep energy flowing.

CRYSTAL SPELL FOR JOYFUL MONEY

When you are starting fresh, either at a new job or a new school, or if you are investing in yourself to begin a new moneymaking endeavor, you will probably experience trepidation or stress. You want to be successful! Sometimes the amount of success you receive is not within your direct sphere of influence. Having a crystal spell to aid your work is an empowering experience. In this spell, the crystal becomes a talisman that you can use to meet your goal and remove the stress that often surrounds money. Basil is an herb associated with happiness, and while it is often said that money cannot buy happiness, by using basil you are establishing a joyful link to money.

Crystal Spell for Joyful Money

You Will Need

- Golden coin, such as a Sacagawea dollar or any legal tender currency coin covered in gold foil (it must be a real coin and not a facsimile)
- 3-inch-diameter circle of yellow cloth
- 1 single crystal, either citrine, heliodor, pyrite, or topaz
- 1 teaspoon dried basil
- 12 inches of metallic gold thread

Directions

1. Place the coin on the cloth. Place the crystal on top of the coin. Sprinkle the basil on top of the crystal and coin.
2. Gather up the edges of the cloth and secure with metallic thread by wrapping the thread around clockwise, leaving a few inches at the two ends to tie together.
3. As money discussions are hard and money is often a source of stress, keep this charm with you to bring joy to your difficult conversations about money. Some scenarios include asking for a raise, interviewing for a school or job, or applying for a loan.

Powering Up for Conversations about Money

If initiating conversations about money causes you stress, try wearing calming crystals that are also associated with communication. Some useful suggestions include chalcedony, turquoise, blue lace agate, and chrysocolla.

CRYSTAL MATRIX FOR GOOD LUCK

Have you ever wondered why horseshoes are considered lucky? Many people believe that it has to do with their shape. The crescent shape has been used in magick for millennia. It is associated with the moon, the goddess, and even protection against evil. Horseshoes are made of iron, and iron is believed to repel demons and unwanted spirits. Horseshoes also have seven holes, and seven is considered an auspicious number because of its numerous associations. You can create a crystal matrix in a horseshoe shape in order to cultivate good luck. The horseshoe shape is like a container that holds the good luck that is coming to you. The open arms pointing up signify your openness to receiving good fortune. Allow good luck to fill your vessel!

This spell uses crystals that focus on good luck regarding money, but for general good luck that is associated with other endeavors and life events that are not directly attached to money, choose a rainbow of crystals such as carnelian, agate, citrine, aventurine, amazonite, lapis lazuli, and amethyst.

Crystal Matrix for Good Luck

You Will Need

- 7 crystals in a variety of colors depending on your purpose (e.g., for good luck surrounding money, you will need 1 of each: pyrite, citrine, amber, aventurine, green fluorite, malachite, and jade)
- Horseshoe (optional)

Directions

1. Place the seven crystals either on top of the horseshoe or in a crescent arrangement on your altar. For good luck in money, alternate the gold and the green crystals. (For a general good luck spell, place them in color order from warm colors to cool colors.) The open ends should be at the top of your arrangement, and the curve of the crescent should be at the bottom.
2. As you place each stone, say an invocation to create the sound vibration that will charge the crystal with good luck. For example,

you may use the following words or create something more specific to your needs:

By the seven seas, good luck flows unto me.
By the seven continents, my good luck is permanent.
By the seven rainbow bands, the best of fortune is at hand.
By the seven days, good luck will stay.
By the seven notes of the scale, good luck will prevail.
By the seven heavens and the seven steps
Good luck flows to me and good luck I accept!

3. Repeat any portion of the charm as you touch each crystal of the crescent. Envision good luck flowing into your crescent or horseshoe and gathering and accumulating. Leave your good luck crystal in a visible place in your environment and visit it whenever you like, touching the crystals when you need an infusion of good luck.

CRYSTAL MATRIX *for* GOOD LUCK

1. Aventurine
2. Pyrite
3. Jade

Manifesting Magick with Crystals

If you want to manifest a new situation, you can use crystals by choosing stones with colors that match your desired situation. Applying for a new job? Look at the company logo of your dream job and include crystals of those colors on your altar. Looking to gain admission to a new school? Match your crystals to the school colors to establish your connection. You can even hold a crystal in your hands and run it through your hair to charge it with your energy and then leave it in a secret place such as a planter on the campus or company where you want to be.

CRYSTAL SPELL FOR BANISHING DEBT

Sometimes your path to success can get cluttered with everything from stumbling blocks to fallow periods where you can't seem to get any traction. Low confidence, repetition of old patterns, and other holdovers can inhibit your progress toward success. One of the hardest things to overcome is debt. Debt grows exponentially on its own. Even if you stop contributing to debt, it will still grow rapidly. Banishing debt requires incredible discipline and luck: two things that crystal magick also requires. Build yourself a crystal pathway in order to keep your focus on banishing debt while shifting your energy into manifesting abundance.

In witchcraft, you might often hear about the spell designed to "release what no longer serves you," and there is perhaps no more necessary application of this paradigm than the release of debt. This doesn't mean that you abdicate responsibility for any accounts that you owe, nor does it mean that you stop paying. This is not a directive to ruin your credit rating by behaving irresponsibly. Using crystals in a debt-banishing spell will help strengthen your resolve, force you to examine patterns, and most importantly, forge new paths that will take you from in the red to in the black.

Crystal Spell for Banishing Debt

You Will Need

- 3 red carnelian or agate crystals (tumbled stones with smooth surfaces are best)
- 3 black obsidian crystals
- Charger or plate to catch wax drippings
- Green taper candle
- Grimoire, journal, or notebook
- Pen

Directions

1. Clear all six crystals, either by smoke, water, or sound.
2. Sit in a quiet place of contemplation. Hold the three red crystals in your hand. Give each one a specific name, such as "credit card debt" or "owed to a friend" or "loan outstanding." Whatever it is that has you in the red, be specific and name each one. Then place the crystals horizontally on the charger.

3. Light the green candle and invoke new beginnings that are specific to your needs. For example, you could say, "As this light dispels the dark, all my debts will soon depart."
4. Hold the black crystals in your hand. Recognize their power to absorb light. Hold each one above the candle flame. You can even quickly pass the crystal through the flame, but you must be quick so that you don't burn your fingers. Allow the energy of your candle invocation to pass into the black crystals one by one. Give the black crystals a charge of their own: "From the dark earth that holds all, contains all, absorbs all, this light is transmuted into power."
5. Allow the green wax to drip all over the red crystals one by one. While the wax is still molten, press the black crystals into the wax so that they are affixed on top of the red crystals. As you do this, imagine yourself moving from the red into the black. Allow the absorptive crystals to transmute the energy of scarcity. Allow the negative energy of negative balances to be absorbed and transformed.
6. Use your grimoire to record the date you performed the spell and the changes that you will make to resolve the situation. It can be small incremental changes, but acting in accord with your spell is important. Word and deed bind the magick. Writing down the actions that you decide to take to change your reality in your grimoire will help you stay accountable to your spell. Some actions may be paying down a balance, limiting new charges, negotiating with collectors to settle old debts, or applying for debt forgiveness. No matter the action, use the crystals to help you focus. Move from red to black.
7. As you complete each action, remove one of the crystal pairs and separate them. Then you can cleanse them and dedicate them to a new purpose.

Clarity Seeking

If you are attempting spells of increase or debt banishing, you may want to consider working with revealer crystals first. Clarity is a necessary first step because wealth can easily be confused with scarcity. If you are seeking only the expensive trappings of material wealth, many times these are not representative of wealth at all. They may appear as indicators of wealth but what they actually are in reality is more debt. Do not confuse debt with wealth. Using crystals for clarity can help you discern and define what true wealth actually is.

Chapter 5

CRYSTALS for HEALING

In a magickal context, healing is a complex subject to engage in. Poor health and emotional injuries are but a few of the challenges that can dominate the human condition. Here you will learn how to channel healing energy through crystals.

USING CRYSTALS FOR HEALING

Healing is a cumulative process, one that you are not always in control of. However, you will find that crystals can be a powerful healing aid because of their inherent beauty and mutability. Many crystals are pseudomorphs, meaning that they retain their crystal structure but can change their chemical composition. There is perhaps no stronger connection between healing and crystals than the mere existence of pseudomorphs—they are proof that change and transformation are possible. You can use this quality to your advantage in your spells. A crystal can help you apply the principles of change in order to move from pain to ease or from distress to peace. The aspect of crystal magick that makes it a valid part of healing is that the magick is connected to some kind of ritual. It is the ritual use of crystals that unlocks their healing power. A lot of how you feel, whether physically or emotionally, has to do with your actions and your attitude toward yourself. Crystals will not cure a serious illness, but using crystals in magick can absolutely impact how you perceive your experience. Pain that is experienced as a passing sensation that you are in control of dissipating rather than as a permanent experience can be attained through working with crystals. This is because the *work* itself creates new neural pathways in your brain: Rituals crafted with healing in mind will never hurt you. At their worst, they will do nothing, and at their best, they will assist your brain in releasing important chemicals such as dopamine and endorphins that will make you feel physically and emotionally better.

These are the crystals used most often in spells for healing:

- Amazonite
- Amber
- Amethyst
- Aquamarine
- Azurite
- Celestite
- Chrysocolla
- Clear quartz
- Emerald
- Fluorite
- Hematite
- Kyanite
- Lapis lazuli
- Malachite
- Moonstone
- Obsidian
- Rhodochrosite
- Rose quartz
- Selenite
- Sodalite
- Sunstone

CRYSTAL HEALING AND THE MIND

In conventional medicine, a treatment's efficacy often depends on how it performs when compared to a placebo. The placebo often does not have any medical benefit, but it still works. In some cases, placebos have worked at a rate of 50 percent, meaning half of the people enrolled in those studies were able to essentially be the source of their own relief. Further investigation reveals that it is not just a fake pill or a belief in healing that leads placebos to work. The surprising success rate of placebos lies in many factors, not the least of which is the act of taking the pill and the fact that the test subjects were receiving attention and care. It is the rituals surrounding the placebos that are a part of their efficacy. It is an object combined with action combined with expectation.

Now imagine that instead of a worthless pill, you are using a natural mineral from the beautiful and powerful capabilities of the crystalline planet, the life-giving force that constantly surrounds you, cradles you, holds all of your accomplishments and ancestors. Imagine holding this powerful tool as you create rituals specific to your needs that you can repeat, strengthen, and imbue with intention, rituals designed to give you pleasure and fuel your healing, leaving you radiant and whole. Building crystal rituals of wellness will only lead you to improved healing. There is no other path that it can take. Some cultures even prescribe crystals of a specific type and size in order to address certain ailments.

CRYSTAL WATER INDRINKING SPELL

Crystal water bottles are a popular accessory among more than just modern witches. A crystal water bottle is a perfect example of simple contagious magick. The water that is in contact with the crystal is affected and changed by the presence of the crystal and becomes infused with the energetic signature of the mineral. Drinking the water transfers the power of the crystal into the person imbibing the infused water. By the law of contact, the crystal will continue to act through the medium of the water. In witchcraft, an indrinking spell involves consuming a potion that is prepared with a particular intention or desired result in mind. By ritualizing the act of creating a potion and including crystals in the spell, you can literally drink in healing energy and allow its transformative powers to course through your body.

This spell calls for a water bottle fitted with a crystal holder. There are several iterations of this product, some that can hold a single medium-sized crystal point and some that can hold tumbled stones and chips. However, it is not necessary to buy a fancy water bottle for this spell. You can use any bottle with a mouth large enough to accommodate your crystal or crystals.

Crystal Water Indrinking Spell

You Will Need

- Crystal of your choosing, selected with intention (e.g., amethyst for a detox, obsidian for protection against illness, moonstone for mental health)
- Water bottle
- Potable water, either filtered water or spring water
- Thin metal straw (optional)

Directions

1. Choose your crystal and set your intention. Wash the crystal under running water as you speak aloud its dedication to the purpose of the spell. For example:

   This amethyst is cleansed. By my intention, it shall assist me in detoxing.

   Or

   Obsidian, dark and pure, protect me so that my health is shielded by your power.

   Or

   Moonstone, bright and glowing, ease my mind with the power of your vibrational energy.

   Feel free to adapt and adjust the type of crystal or the language to suit your immediate purpose.
2. Place the crystal in the bottle or secure it in the crystal holder and fill the bottle with potable water.
3. Focus your attention on the crystal as you envision the effects of your spoken charm diffusing through the water.

4. Speak the charm (or any variation of the charms suggested above that resonate with you) three times into the water while you are looking at the crystals at the bottom of the bottle. Bring your mouth close enough that you can see the vibration of your words on the surface of the water.
5. Drink the water and take the intention amplified by the crystal energy into your body. If your water container does not have a chamber or holder to secure your crystals, use the straw to drink all the water.

Creative Crystal Bath Altar

You can also use crystals in a ritual bath by creating a crystal altar using a shelf that can span the width of your bathtub, or you can use a small folding tray to keep within reach. To add to the relaxing atmosphere, add some candles for a truly transformative experience.

CRYSTAL HEALING RESTORATIVE MINERAL BATH

Crystals are minerals, and your body needs minerals in order to function properly. Mineral deficiencies can lead to low energy and discomfort. Fortunately, certain necessary minerals can be absorbed through the skin. By adding crystals to a restorative mineral bath, you can create a ritual of healing that will impact your state of mind as well as your corporeal form. Crystals add a layer of magick to your self-care routine. Using crystals in a mineral bath can and will augment the benefits of this healing ritual.

Crystal Healing Restorative Mineral Bath

You Will Need

- 3 tumbled crystals: carnelian to improve vitality, bloodstone for purification and renewal, and celestite for calming
- ¼ cup coarse sea salt
- 1 teaspoon sulfur crystals
- 2 cups magnesium bath crystals or Epsom salts
- 3-cup (or 24-ounce) container with a tight-fitting lid
- 3–5 drops lavender essential oil

Directions

1. Combine the three crystals, sea salt, sulfur crystals, and magnesium bath crystals in the container.
2. Add the lavender oil. Secure the lid of the container.
3. Start running a hot bath, as warm as you can comfortably tolerate. As the bath fills, gently shake the container to mix all of the ingredients.
4. Take handfuls of the mixture and add it to the bath.
5. Hold the three crystals in your hand and use your hand to stir the bath water so that the minerals dissolve.
6. Get in the bath and lie back so that you can place the three crystals directly on your body on or around your heart, solar plexus, and abdomen. Allow the dissolved minerals to give you some buoyancy. You might feel your hands floating up as you relax. Let them.
7. Place the soles of your feet together and let your knees fall away from each other if that movement is available to you.
8. Keeping your face above the water, let your head sink enough that the water fills your ears. Breathe deeply and close your eyes, allowing your mind to be clear. Focus on the vibrations through the water. You will experience sound differently. Feel your body absorb the minerals through your skin as you enjoy the warm water.
9. Stay in the bath as long as you're comfortable and then emerge restored and willing to accept the benefits of the ritual bath.

A Shower of Crystals

If you don't have time for a long ritual bath, you can still receive the energy of crystals by placing a few crystals in a muslin pouch or a tea strainer and hanging it from your showerhead so that the water passes through the crystals as you shower.

CRYSTAL MINDFULNESS MENDING RITUAL

Some of the most frequent uses of crystals are to induce, enhance, or contribute to a state of calm. There is an undeniable connection between your mood and your performance. Mindset affects everything from interpersonal interactions to how you feel about yourself. Clearing the mind and actively seeking peace is a worthwhile endeavor that numerous crystals are well suited for. Here is a simple crystal spell for cultivating mindfulness.

Crystal Mindfulness Mending Ritual

You Will Need

- Serene and quiet place to reflect
- Medium (approximately 1-inch) tumbled crystal (lapis lazuli, sodalite, or azurite)

Directions

1. Cultivate peace in your environment by turning off your phone and sitting in a comfortable position. Try a lotus position if you are able to. Hold the crystal in your left hand with your palm facing up. Place your right hand over your left hand.
2. Take a deep breath and notice the temperature of the crystal. Concentrate on its shape and its weight. Pressing the crystal gently between your palms, move your hands in a small circle across one another. Feel the temperature of the crystal adjust to your body temperature.
3. Hold the crystal in your dominant hand and bring it up to your forehead, holding it about an inch above the bridge of your nose, between your eyes. Press gently to hold the stone in place and take a deep breath. Experience the texture of the crystal against your third eye.
4. Allow your mind to focus just on the sensation of breath and the crystal against your skin. Clear your mind of random thoughts, being fully present in the here and now, attuning your focus to a simple act of connecting to crystal energy through breath. Allow all else to fall away.
5. Remain in this relaxed but alert and observant state for as long as you need until you feel that you have received the benefit.

EMOTIONAL RENEWAL WITH CRYSTALS

While contentment is an emotion that is generally acceptable to express, the range of human emotions contains many soaring heights and some deep depths, and many emotions can lead you into a disturbed state. Anger, frustration, and confusion are some of the emotions that can result from the many micro-confrontations that you will encounter in daily life.

Interactions with people, events that go wrong, and miscommunications can all be challenging and draining, and may take a toll on your emotional state, which is going to affect your magick. In order to address emotional upsets, you can use crystals to bring you back into a balanced state. A state of balance is not synonymous with contentment. Society gets concerned when people express anything other than happiness, but all emotions are important because they are all signs that you need to pay attention to. When you are feeling angry, it is most likely because someone has crossed a boundary and violated you in some way. Gossip, or the feeling of being talked about, can induce paranoia when you start to wonder what people might be saying about you. You can allow yourself to feel your emotions and integrate them. You do not have to deny your emotions, but you also do not need to be ruled by them.

You will need a power pack of working crystals to help you get back to center and secure your power over your emotional state. Here are some suggestions:

- **Confronting Sadness:** Try selenite and obsidian. Let the powers of light and darkness guide you to a state of balance. Keep one crystal in each hand and then switch them every time you feel a shift in your emotions.
- **Addressing Anger:** Try carnelian and celestite. Let the fiery power of carnelian get your blood pumping while celestite allows you to transcend the throes of anger. Hold both crystals in your dominant hand and squeeze your hand and allow yourself space to accept righteous anger as you envision new and stronger boundaries.
- **Resolving Confusion:** Try clear quartz and amazonite. Truth, hope, healing, and clarity will help you cut through any misunderstandings or miscommunications. With a crystal in each hand, bring your hands together with your palms touching. Press the heels of your hands and your fingertips together, keeping the crystals in place. Feel the opening around the crystals as you make space for clarity. Keep your fingers rigid as you envision cutting through all the nonsense.

HEALING GENERATIONAL WOUNDS

Sometimes the challenges you face are not of your making, but rather you are carrying the painful energy signatures of a distant past that formed your present, even though it may be unknown to you. Tap into the ancient nature of crystals to connect you with the past. They will guide you exactly where you need to go. Crystals have been around for millions of years. They have seen every dashed hope, every descendant from every lineage on every continent except Antarctica. And crystals are tangible proof of change. Because crystals have unique properties and unique energy signatures, it is possible to use all of their attributes for accelerating healing that reaches far beyond the present moment. Crystals by nature of their existence are proof of transformation. This transformation occurs because of two things: water and time. This generational crystal healing spell uses both of these with a few additions.

In this spell you will need three crystals. You will choose these crystals based on what you know about yourself and your lineage. Each one represents a different generation of your ancestry. Go back as far as you need so that you may uncover and reveal the original wound that is informing your present. Choose your crystals by consulting the information in Part 2 and find a crystal that you know to have been discovered in or around one of your ancestral lands. This crystal will represent your distant ancestors. The next crystal will represent the generations that have immediately preceded you. Consider migrations of your grandparents or great-grandparents and choose a crystal that hails from their journey's end, not its beginning. Finally, the third crystal will represent you. Refer to some of the tables in Chapter 10 to choose an identity crystal for this spell. Here's an example:

- Your ancestors immigrated to the United States from Brazil. Choose amethyst to represent the distant ancestral lines because Brazil is a major source of amethyst.
- You grew up in Florida and your parents still live there. Choose moonstone, as it is the state gem of Florida, to represent the preceding generations.
- You were born in March, so choose aquamarine to represent yourself.

Spell to Heal Generational Wounds

You Will Need

- Clear glass jar approximately 32 ounces (or any jar large enough to accommodate your crystals with a mouth wide enough for you to reach in easily)
- Spring water or purified water, enough to fill the jar ⅔ full
- Tea light candle or floating candle
- Stick of incense (optional)
- 3 crystals (1 to represent the distant past, 1 to represent the recent past, and 1 to represent the present)
- Small towel or washcloth
- Additional crystals (1 each of malachite, azurite, amazonite, rose quartz, hematite)

Directions

1. Fill the jar with water and place the jar in front of you. Light the candle and place it behind the jar. Light the incense, if this calls to you, and place it to the right of the jar.
2. Take the crystals you have chosen and place them in front of you in the following order: Right: the crystal representing the distant past. Center: the crystal representing the generations preceding you. Left: the crystal representing your current self or your current family.
3. Take the crystal on the right and hold it in your hands. Allow the crystal to tell you its story. Listen to it. The voices of your ancestors are speaking through it. Allow space for their pain. You may hear upsetting things such as enslavement, peril, separation, and traumatic death. Hold this crystal and make space for the hurt that has occurred and has traveled. Place this crystal in the water.
4. Take the second crystal in your hand and repeat the process of quiet listening. You may hear of struggle—economic, social, or otherwise. You may hear of unwilling motherhood or loss of stability. You have already gone very far back and are now getting closer to how all of these traumas of the past are informing your present. Make space for them to be seen and acknowledged. Then put the second crystal in the jar of water along with the first.
5. Take the final crystal and allow yourself to feel the culmination of all of the wrongs inflicted, endured, or caused in the past. Feel the impact and understand that it is now your sacred duty to transform the past

into the present so that the wound can heal. Place your crystal in the water.

6. Place the towel in front of you and make a square matrix in front of the jar using the malachite, the azurite, the amazonite, and the rose quartz.
7. Take the first, ancestral crystal out of the jar and put it in the center of the four-way matrix. Take the malachite and touch it to this crystal, focusing on the following truth: Malachite by its nature contains the power to transform. Its green healing energy transforms this past wound, no matter how ancient or deep, into a new realm of healing. Put the malachite back in its corner.
8. Take the azurite and touch it to the ancestral crystal. Focus on this next truth: Azurite brings an intense calm and accelerates healing. It is a stone of expansion, and it is a companion to malachite. Together, they are working to expand the opening in the field of time, and allowing space for healing to grow. Put the azurite back in its corner of the grid.
9. Take the amazonite and touch it to the ancestral crystal while focusing on this truth: Amazonite is a revealer of truth. Family secrets can be uncovered without shame, and forgiveness is offered to all who deserve it or require it for the elevation of their soul. Put the amazonite back in its place.
10. Take the rose quartz and touch it to the ancestral crystal while focusing on this truth: Rose quartz represents the heart that is whole and joyful. Surround your ancestors with love. Then return the rose quartz to its original place in the matrix.
11. Now take the next crystal out of the jar, the one that represents the generation(s) just preceding you. Place it to the right of the ancestral crystal and repeat the process, touching each crystal from the square grid to the stone and reflecting on the attributes of each crystal.
12. Finally, take the crystal representing you out of the water and perform the ritual for the third time, touching each crystal and accepting the gifts of transformative healing, forgiveness, truth, and love for yourself. Place this crystal to the right of the generational stone.
13. You should now have what looks like a line of stones from left to right inside of a square grid. You have rewritten your story by reversing the order of the crystals. You have cleansed the past and the present

by briefly immersing the crystals in water. And you have blessed them all with powerful healing energy.

14. Take the hematite and allow yourself time to reflect and ground your energy. Confronting the wounds of the past is emotionally fraught work. Be gentle with yourself and allow any feelings of upset to pass through you into the hematite, then place it on the ground or floor.
15. Blow out the candle and pour the water into the earth or into a houseplant. Keep the crystals nearby if they bring you comfort. If your work is done, at least for now, you may put them away until you have need of them again.

Crystals and Water

While water is essential for cleaning and clearing most crystals, softer crystals can be damaged when exposed to water for long periods of time. Malachite, hematite, fluorite, and selenite are among the softer crystals that can be damaged by long exposure to water. A good rule to remember is that if your crystal ends with the suffix "—ite," then you should use only the cleaning and clearing spells where exposure to water is minimal.

RESTORING THE SPIRIT

Crystals in healing magick are soothing to the mind and body. The spirit is connected to, but separate from, the mind and body. These three forms of consciousness—corporeal, mental, and spiritual—are the gateways through which you experience life itself. Calm and untroubled minds lead to better physical health because that sense of peace can translate into fewer accidents and less stress. Stress takes a toll on the body, and the body keeps score. This is not meant to suggest that crystals will be effective in treating a serious illness, nor are they a substitute for medical advice, but anyone confronting ill health can and will benefit from mental stamina. And because the mind, body, and spirit are connected, caring for the body and the mind will also strengthen the spirit. You have already learned a few ways to use crystals in restoring the body and attuning the mind. You can also use them to elevate your spirit.

Restoring the Spirit

You Will Need

- Selenite
- Celestite or fluorite
- Moonstone
- Sunstone or heliodor

Directions

1. If you are able to, sit comfortably on a mat with your spine straight. Hold the crystals in your hand. In front of you, place the selenite. Do this slowly and mindfully, focused on spiritual ascension. Behind you, place the celestite (or substitute fluorite). To the left of you, place the moonstone. To the right, place the sunstone (or substitute heliodor).
2. Envision threads of light emanating from the crystals and traveling upward until all four converge at a point a few inches above the crown of your skull. Close your eyes and focus on that point just above where your corporeal body ends. At this point, you might feel a tingling sensation encircling your head. Now summon the electricity that is already circulating in your body and see if you can focus this energy in the same exact spot. Allow the sensation of gathering energy to grow.
3. Next, return your focus to the place where the energy threads of the crystals meet. See if you can bridge the small gap between the corporeal energy you have summoned from within yourself and join it to the power you are drawing forth from the crystals.
4. Once the visualization is clear in your mind and you feel that heightening of spiritual energy, take the mental construct of yourself, radiant and energized and seated in the center of a pyramidal light structure, and duplicate the entire image and then invert it. You are now envisioning yourself floating in the center of a lattice of light. You are contained within a dipyramidal dodecahedron. It is as though you are in the center of a square that forms the base of a pyramid of light. The apex of the pyramid is directly above your head. The same structure of light is below you, only it is upside down because the square you are occupying with your energy is the base of this pyramid too. It extends below you with the apex directly underneath you. You are at the center and you are the balance point.
5. Your next task is to harmonize within the sacred geometry and allow it to support you. One point of the pyramid is directed to the heavens

up above. Underneath you is a point that extends below the earth. You have joined your energy with both of these points. Now you may travel between them.

6. Focus on the point above you where you have touched the metaphysical energetic meeting point of the mental crystal structure. Amplify your energy into this point and send it skyward as though a silver cord were emanating from the top of your head and you could travel along this cord.
7. Repeat this exercise, only in the inverse so that the cord you are envisioning also extends below you into the earth. Send energy in this direction to ground yourself.
8. Enjoy the enlivenment of being in a balanced state and spiritually aware. Let a sense of connectedness and peace travel through you.
9. Slowly envision the energy traveling back to you through the cords. You are drawing energy up from the earth and downloading it from the heavens. Integrate the energy into your spirit body by picturing your heart center as the meeting point of both of the cords of energy and light.
10. Begin to dismantle the mental construct of the double pyramid one thread at a time by drawing the threads into your consciousness. Envision each plane permeating your consciousness like a retractable tape measure returning to its casing.
11. Once you have received the invigorating spiritual boost of creative visualization, pick up the crystals and hold them in your hands: moonstone and selenite in your left hand and celestite and sunstone in your right hand.
12. Breathe deeply as you return to the here and now. Keep the idea of the four crystals as a portable spiritual sanctuary that you can tap into just by touching them and reminding yourself of the peace and power you can create with them.

HEART HEALING

There is perhaps nothing more indicative of wellness than a happy heart. Happiness is a preferred state of emotion, yet it can often feel far away, especially when your heart is wounded. Kindness is not always reciprocated. Trust is not always deserved. Promises can be broken, disappointments can pile up, and often these can result in heart wounds that can be difficult to bear.

Using crystals in matters of the heart is a way of taking positive action. Crystals are keepers of the secrets of the earth. They form under intense pressure. They can absorb and transform anything that you have carried long enough and are ready to let go of in order to make space for something new. Use crystals to accentuate the process of healing from heartbreak.

Spell to Heal from Heartbreak

You Will Need

- Small (1½- to 2-inch) crystal sphere
- Rose quartz tower
- Small votive candle, either pink or white

Directions

1. On your altar, place the three items in the following arrangement: the sphere closest to you, the tower behind the sphere, the candle in between the tower and the sphere.
2. Once you have arranged the crystals, light the candle.
3. Pick up the sphere and use it to focus. A crystal sphere is the heart of the crystal. Hold it to your heart and see if you can get to the heart of the matter, the root cause of your heart's unease, no matter how heavy it feels or how hard it might be to let go (for example, feelings of unworthiness, feelings of loneliness, feelings of disappointment).
4. Gently pressing the sphere against your heart, start to gently move it in a counterclockwise motion. By moving the crystal widdershins, you are reversing or undoing the unease. When you feel that you are ready to change, pause and touch the crystal to the top of the tower, allowing it to infuse with radiant, loving energy. Then apply the crystal to your heart again and reverse the direction so that you are moving it clockwise.
5. Allow a tower of love and sweetness to permeate your heart. Understand that while you may not always be in control of your emotions, you are in control of your witchcraft and you have the power to turn things around.
6. Place the sphere in front of the candle and enjoy the light moving through it. Picture the light moving through your heart, illuminating its chambers and dispelling the darkness.

7. When you feel like it, blow out the candle and do something that brings you pleasure, no matter how small.

The Right Time for Healing

If the emotional wound is deep, you may wish to do a healing spell on a full moon to take in as much magick as you can. Tuesdays are also auspicious for healing. Sacred to the Norse god Tyr, some of the magickal associations with Tuesday include justice, strength, and physical well-being.

Chapter 6

CRYSTAL CHARMS for LOVE

Love and the desire for love are often what bring practitioners into witchcraft. There are many crystals associated with love, including rose quartz, aventurine, jade, garnet, and rhodochrosite. If you are looking to use crystals to improve relationships, strengthen bonds, support emotional healing, and promote peace, you will find many suitable applications in this chapter. If you are looking to manipulate someone into reciprocating your affections against their free will, you will find nothing of use here because crystal magick is a type of geomancy, or earth magick, and not alchemy. Crystal magick will not alter one type of relationship by changing it into another, but crystal magick can assist love relationships that are going through an evolution or change by addressing the emotional, spiritual, and mental well-being of the people participating in the relationship.

USING CRYSTALS FOR LOVE

Because of their inherent beauty, their sensuality, and their unique abilities to provide a sense of calm, crystals can be used in attracting, deepening, and awakening many different types of love. Bonds of friendship and family, self-love, romantic love, and sensual love can all be amplified with crystal magick. Crystals can also be included in your own practice of elevating your confidence in order to attract or manifest a desired outcome.

Greek philosophy is famed for its seven delineations of the types of love, and every type has a crystal correspondence that you can explore. Eros in the modern sense is understood to be the embodiment of erotic love but has its philosophical roots in friendship, enthusiasm, and the love of knowledge. Eros is considered the "driving love." Crystals of passion and vitality can help you attune to this type of love. In contrast, philia is a type of committed love. Where eros is ambitious and fiery, philia is more tempered and lasting but just as intimate. Grounding crystals and calming crystals can be used to accentuate a lasting and committed love. Agape has come to be understood as a type of selfless love, or love of all people that extends even to those unknown to you. It represents an intense fondness and is no less sincere even though its philosophical history is not connected to intimacy. Transforming crystals and those associated with spiritual awakening are useful to help you tap into universal love.

These are the crystals used most often in spells for love:

- Amazonite
- Aventurine
- Emerald
- Garnet
- Jade
- Kunzite
- Lapis lazuli
- Moonstone
- Peridot
- Rhodochrosite
- Rhodolite
- Rose quartz
- Ruby

CRYSTAL WITCH SELF-LOVE SPELL

The mere concept of self-love can be foreign to some. Self-love has a lot of negative associations attached to it. Personality traits such as arrogance, self-centeredness, vanity, and pride can make it difficult to sustain healthy relationships. Conversely, low self-esteem, a lack of confidence, and self-deprecation can also inhibit your ability to bond. For these reasons, consider self-love to be a *part* of all healthy relationships, starting with your own relationship with yourself. You want to achieve a balance of being proud of your accomplishments and secure in your abilities while also understanding that you are worthy of love—that you have innate value. A lot of witches struggle with the concept of self-love. Even the word "witch" has a lot of negative connotations among people. Loving your witch identity and loving your craft, feeling secure in your choices and empowered in your path and your spells, goes a long way toward amplifying and accelerating magick. In Wicca, there is a tenet among coven members that requires them to meet in "perfect love and perfect trust." In this ritual, you will meet yourself as a crystal witch in perfect love and perfect trust.

Spell to Amplify Self-Love

In this spell you will need a crystal that represents your strength in witchcraft. Some examples of this might be moonstone if you are clairvoyant, charoite if you are adept at ritual and work as a high priestess or priest, amazonite if you are a healer, amethyst if you can astral project, or obsidian or malachite if you are a hex breaker. If you are not certain what your strength as a witch is, choose an aspirational crystal that represents the ability or skill that you plan to cultivate.

You Will Need

- Crystal that represents your identity from the activity in Chapter 10—this can be your birthstone crystal, your zodiac correspondence crystal, or an adjacent zodiac crystal
- Crystal to represent love (choose rose quartz, emerald, or aventurine, whichever you resonate with the most strongly)
- Crystal to represent your strength in witchcraft

Directions

1. On your altar, place the three crystals. You will name them and speak their names as a charm to imbue them with intention as you place them from right, to left, and then center, above the first two. Call them by name according to the following list:

My power to my right (this is the crystal that represents your witchy ability).
My heart to my left (this is the rose quartz, emerald, or aventurine).
Myself at the cone of power (this crystal represents you).

2. You should be looking at a simple triangle matrix with your identity crystal at the apex. Love will be on the left-hand side, and power on the right.
3. Touch the crystal on the left with your left hand and speak the charm:

   I greet myself in perfect love.

4. Touch the crystal on the right with your right hand and speak the charm:

   I trust my own power.

5. Gently move the two crystals toward the apex so that each is touching either side of the crystal that represents you. Hold your hands above the three crystals and speak the charm:

   Love is beside me. Love is within me.
   Power beside me. Power within me.
   Witch of the heart, witch of the mind.
   Trusting and loving, powerful, kind.

6. Pick up the crystal in the center. Give it a kiss. Carry it with you whenever you need a boost of confidence. Return it to your altar whenever you need to recharge it by repeating the spell.

TWIN FLAME REVEALER LOVE SPELL

The concept of a twin flame describes a relationship that is very intense and can feel like stars colliding. A twin flame is someone who impacts your life in a substantial way. Even though a lot of people associate a twin flame with a romantic partner, this is not always the case. It is possible for a twin flame to be a romantic partner, but not every romantic partner will be a twin flame. A twin flame is a person that is more of a catalyst. This is someone whose energy impacts yours in a highly intense, illuminating way. Think of the relationship between the sun and the moon. In mythology, these celestial bodies are personified as deities and often they are brother and sister, not lovers. One reflects the light of the other, and in so doing, shines on its own in a truly beautiful and unique way. This is the best way to understand a twin flame. If you think someone might be your twin flame, but you are not sure, you can use crystal divination to get a stronger sense of the nature of the relationship.

Twin Flame Revealer Love Spell

The crystals you choose for this spell should have some magickal connection to each of you and should have some kind of relationship. Choose from the following options, or allow them to inspire you to create your own pairing. For example:

- **Moonstone and labradorite:** Moonstone is light, has adularescence, and appears to glow, while labradorite is dark, has iridescence, and appears to shine. They are equal opposites. If this describes your relationship, start working with these two crystals.
- **Malachite and azurite:** They are often found together. Malachite is a pseudomorph and can change into the crystal shape of other minerals. Azurite can be affected by the air and is known to change into malachite. If you and your suspected twin flame are inseparable and complete each other's sentences, or people tell you that you look alike, work with malachite and azurite.
- **Amethyst and citrine, or two ametrine crystals:** Amethyst and citrine can grow so close together that sometimes they occupy the same matrix and lattice at the same time. Amethyst is spiritual and cleansing, while citrine is creative and bright. If the two of you are so like-minded that you rarely disagree, or like the same things but have different opinions about them, consider working with these crystals.

You Will Need

- Crystal pendulum
- 2 crystals, 1 to represent you and 1 to represent the other person

Directions

1. Try sitting on the floor (if that is available to you) in front of your altar and place the two crystals in front of you. Touch the crystals

and speak their names. For example, one you would call by your own name, and the other you would call your twin flame.

2. Next, calibrate your pendulum by holding it in the balance point between contact, weight, and tension. The tension is in the line. The weight is the crystal that is putting the tension in the line through gravity. And the contact is your voice and the hand that you are holding the end of the line with. Try to remain absolutely still as you hold the pendulum in your dominant hand so that it is above the crystals that you have chosen to work with.
3. Ask the pendulum to show you "yes." The pendulum will move, and usually it will either rotate, oscillate, or vibrate. Allow time for the movement to become clear. You may have to ask several times ("Show me yes") until you establish an energetic link.
4. Test the clairvoyant connection by taking one of the crystals that have an established relationship, place it directly beneath the pendulum, and say, "This is me." The pendulum will either affirm or deny. If the pendulum denies and you do not get the "yes" movement, take the second crystal and repeat, holding the pendulum over the crystal and saying, "This is me."
5. Once you get an affirmative and you have established communication between the crystal and the pendulum and yourself, move the other crystal underneath the pendulum. This is also helpful because not only are you calibrating the pendulum by getting a clear communication and understanding of what an affirmative answer looks like, you are identifying your role in the relationship as well. The crystals are important because you have chosen them according to their physical nature and their metaphysical characteristics. Twin flame relationships are very close, and this part of the spell will clarify who you are to each other in the relationship. The answer might even surprise you.
6. Next, take as much time as you need to clearly envision the person you think might be your twin flame. You are drawn to this spell because there is someone you have in mind. Picture them in detail: name, age, race, face, height, weight, coloring, and any other identity markers that you can easily conjure.
7. Hold the pendulum over the other crystal (this is the crystal that you did not identify as yourself) and say, "This is my twin flame."
8. If you have calibrated the pendulum and it agrees by showing you an affirmation, you are in a twin flame relationship. If the pendulum

does not affirm your query, this person might not be your twin flame, but you may have some other type of spiritual or soul connection. Remember that a soulmate is not the same thing as a twin flame.

CRYSTAL SOULMATE SPELL

A soulmate is someone that you are bonded to in a spiritual way. This is a romantic relationship accompanied by a deep friendship as well as an intimate or sexual connection. Romantic love and the search for a soulmate is often a starting point of what draws people to magick. As previously stated, it is not really possible to conjure romantic love out of nothing using crystals. Even crystal pseudomorphs have to start with something for transformation to take place. Piezoelectric crystals can amplify a vibration, but they are not the source of the vibration. Pyroelectric crystals can transform heat into vibration, but they are not the source of the heat. And romantic love relationships can flame out quickly if the spark is not tended to lovingly and regularly. Very much like a fire, if you feed romantic love, it has a tendency to grow, but starve it of oxygen and it will go out. Crystal magick is but one source of oxygen to allow your relationship to grow into deep and connected love. Soulmates are believed to travel together through multiple lifetimes with the belief that while the body is temporary, the soul endures and soulmates may find each other and maintain their connection. Connections between people do need maintenance in order to remain strong. This crystal spell is designed to deepen and enhance feelings of love and attachment between partners who believe that they are soulmates.

Crystal Soulmate Spell

You Will Need

- 3 (4-inch) spell candles: pink, green, and white
- Small rose quartz crystal
- Small aventurine crystal
- 1 foot of red cotton thread
- Metal charger or small cast iron skillet
- Dried rose petals and small rosebuds
- Clear quartz crystal, any size
- ¾ cup coarse salt
- Muslin bag or pouch

Directions

1. Take the pink candle and the green candle and hold them together side by side.
2. Place the rose quartz on top of the green candle.
3. Place the aventurine on top of the pink candle.
4. Take the red thread and bind all four items, the two candles and the two crystals, together into one bundle.
5. Place the charger or skillet on your altar. Create a ring of dried rose petals and rosebuds on its outermost edge.
6. Use the clear quartz crystal to trace a circle clockwise three times around the outside of the ring of roses while repeating, "My love is celebrated. My love is beautiful."
7. Next, create a ring of salt inside of the ring of roses so that you have a ring of salt close to the center.
8. Use the clear quartz crystal to trace a circle in the air around this inner ring, saying, "My love is protected. My love is pure."
9. Light the white candle and allow the wax to drip into a small pool in the very center of the charger or skillet. When enough has accumulated, place the pink and green candles with their bound crystals in the molten wax puddle and hold them there while it cools.
10. While you wait for the wax to solidify, hold the clear crystal in the hand that is not securing the crystals and candles bundle to the wax and repeat, "My love is centered. My love is strong," until the wax has cooled and the bundle is firmly set.
11. Light the pink and green candles from the white candle. Blow out the white candle and allow the pink and green candles to burn down while you speak or meditate on the following aspects:

    My soulmate (you can use your partner's name) and I are bonded.
    My soulmate and I are in love.
    My soulmate and I are enlightened.
    As it is both below and above.
    My soulmate and I are passionate.
    Together, we are magick and strong
    Together we face whatever may come
    Faithful and constant, lifelong.

12. Allow the candles to burn down. When the candles are spent and the pools of wax have cooled, retrieve the crystals and pick off the wax

and give them a cleaning. (No need to clear them because they are imbued with loving energy.)

13. Gather up the salt and roses and place them in a muslin bag or pouch for when you need to recharge.
14. Give one crystal to your partner and keep the other one for yourself. Add your crystal to the pouch whenever you need to recharge it.

Crystal Clear Consent

While witchcraft is not dogmatic and does not adhere to a single set of published tenets among traditions, it is generally considered a best practice of magick to only work magick involving other people when they have agreed to it. If you want to do a love spell, check in with your partner to get their consent in the magickal undertaking before you begin.

CRYSTAL PASSION SPELL

Crystals are tactile and colorful, which makes them inherently sensual. You can use these same properties to augment passion in your relationships. Whether you want to celebrate, inspire, or rekindle passion, crystals can help. Crystals invite touch, and touch is a powerful connection in love. Touch can be affectionate, giving pleasure and receiving pleasure. Passion is often metaphorically described as a fire or a fever. For this reason, stones such as garnet, ruby, chalcedony, citrine, and sunstone are used in love magick intended to inspire or augment passion. Many crystals also have twinning planes where two crystal have a "touch point" or are originating from the exact same plane. Finding a twin crystal cluster is auspicious for this type of magick. If a twin crystal is available to you, you can use it for the Crystal Passion Spell. If a twin crystal is not available to you, substitute two crystal points and arrange them so that they are touching.

Crystal Passion Spell

You can do this spell alone or together with a partner. You may also substitute your lover's name as you speak the charms.

You Will Need

- Red spell candle
- Twin crystal or 2 crystal points
- Red garnet crystal, rhodolite, or ruby to represent passion
- Citrine for enthusiasm and playfulness
- Labradorite or sunstone to represent heat

Directions

1. Set up your spell in a place where you experience or want to experience sensual intimacy. Light the red candle and put the twin crystal (or crystal points, touching) in front of it.
2. Pick up the garnet and quickly pass it through the candle flame. Bring the crystal to your lips and recite the charm:

   Bring me this and only this
   Crystal and fire in your kiss.

3. Pass the garnet through the flame again and then bring it to your heart, holding it against your skin. Say:

   By the crystal passion's flame
   My heart is wild and calls your name.

4. Pass the garnet through the flame for the third time, allow it to cool for a few seconds, and hold it against your abdomen 3 inches below your navel, making sure the crystal is coming into contact with your skin. Say:

   For the one I love so much
   Feel the passion in my touch.

5. Place the garnet so that it is touching the twin crystal.
6. Pick up the citrine and pass it quickly through the candle flame, then hold it to your third eye. Speak the charm:

   By this citrine and the sun
   In you, I find delight and fun.

7. Pass the citrine through the candle again, then bring it to your lips and speak the charm:

   Where the sweetest honey drips
   I find passion on your lips.

8. Make one last pass through the flame with the citrine, then hold it against your sacral chakra and recite the charm:

   In the place where bodies meet
   I give and I accept your heat.

9. Place the citrine next to the garnet so that they are both touching the twin crystal.
10. Take the labradorite in your hands. Close your eyes and try to get in touch with your intuition and take several deep breaths while holding the crystal. You will use it to do an aura cleansing.
11. Pass the labradorite through the candle flame three times, and instead of speaking a charm, use the labradorite to communicate through touch. Touch the labradorite to the back of your hand and trace it up your arm, across your chest, and down your other arm. Notice the sensations and pay attention to any heightened sensory awareness that you might be feeling.
12. Starting at your chin, trace a line down the midline of your body with the labradorite. Touch any other parts of your body that are asking for attention. When you are finished, place the labradorite next to the other crystals and blow the candle out.
13. Relax and enjoy being at home in your body and all the pleasures that come with being alive.

Crystal Pleasures

Pleasure wands made from crystals are frequently sold for intimate use. There has been some question about their hygienic safety, so it is worth mentioning that quartz family crystals such as clear quartz, rose quartz, amethyst, and citrine are nonporous crystals and can be safely used intimately provided that they are cared for and stored properly and washed with mild soap and water after use.

PHILIA: CRYSTAL SPELL FOR FRIENDSHIP

So much emphasis and excitement surrounds romance and sex that it is easy to forget that friendships need nurturing too. Using crystals can reinforce these bonds, provide a point of common interest, and be an engaging topic of conversation. Sharing crystals between friends is a lovely way to express the bond of an important relationship.

Crystal Spell for Friendship

You Will Need

- 2 prasiolite crystals
- 2 lapis lazuli crystals
- 2 rose quartz crystals
- 2 sunstone crystals (or golden beryl/heliodor)
- 2 sapphire (blue) crystals
- 2 small muslin or velvet pouches
- Your birthstone or zodiac crystal
- Birthstone or zodiac crystal of your beloved friend

Directions

1. Place the crystals in two lines, one type of crystal in each line. Each crystal is a gift. Name each crystal according to its purpose, such as:
    - A gift of prasiolite for growth and new adventures
    - A gift of lapis lazuli for the power of friendship and of respect
    - A gift of rose quartz for unconditional love
    - A gift of sunstone for lightness and fun
    - A gift of sapphire for loyalty and trust
2. Place the crystals in the pouches, five in each. Then add your birthstone to one pouch and your friend's crystal to the other pouch.
3. Give the crystal pouch with your birthstone to your friend and keep the pouch with their birthstone with you. You can even trade back and forth for those moments when you need your friend to remind you of your own personal worth and strength.

CRYSTAL AGAPE SPELL FOR THE LOVE OF ALL PEOPLE

Agape is a form of profound spiritual love that has its origins in ancient Greek philosophy and is still used to describe deified love in modern religion. Agape is considered a transcendent love and one of the highest forms of love. Expressing love for all people can be especially challenging if you are navigating from a place of pain. Unfortunately, people on the planet Earth have a lengthy history of being particularly terrible to each other, and it does not always feel possible to extend feelings of love to all people.

The world population is divided and categorized in many ways: by race, by class, by religious beliefs, and by gender constructs. These delineations can inflame negative feelings, as unresolved traumas and injustices impact how groups of people see and interact with each other. Loving fellow humans can feel like an impossible and improbable task. Crystal magick can bring you a sense of peace as you attempt to form bonds of forgiveness and acceptance for people, all people, even those you disagree with. This spell is especially helpful when recovering from direct action or activism when you may have encountered confrontation and opposition.

Crystal Agape Spell for the Love of All People

You Will Need

- Hematite for grounding
- Lapis lazuli for heart expanding
- Aventurine or jade for heart opening
- Onyx for protection

Directions

1. Gather the four crystals and sit in a comfortable position.
2. Arrange the crystals on your altar or in front of you in a simple four-way matrix with the hematite closest to you, the lapis lazuli farthest from you, the aventurine or jade on the left, and the onyx on the right.
3. Take the hematite and hold it to your heart. Project your energy into the crystal and allow the hematite to absorb it. Here, you are releasing your frustration and blocks, those obstacles that are in the way of forgiveness and communication. Breathe into your emotions and allow them to transfer into the hematite. Then place it on the floor.
4. Next, take the onyx and hold it in front of, but not to, your heart. Envision its energy expanding to surround you like a shield. Any negativity that is coming at you is being absorbed and it is not reaching you. Ideological differences, political differences, religious differences, all the disconnects that separate you from others and all the discord that the separation creates is absorbed by the onyx and does not touch you. When you have a vision of the emotional fallout being stopped by the shield, place the onyx on the ground.

5. Next, take the aventurine and hold it to your heart. Allow its creative, green energy to create space for something new: a new understanding, or compassion, acceptance, or forgiveness (if it is deserved). Feel your heart open to new pathways of compassion and find this connection within yourself. Renew your heart with deep breaths. Keep your eyes closed if that helps you focus. Place the aventurine back on your altar or in its original place.
6. Finally, take the lapis lazuli and touch it to your third eye (on your forehead between and above your eyebrows). Envision the crystal opening a portal to your mind, and through this portal, you are sending out powerful loving vibrations capable of opening the minds of others. Experience the crystal as an open door that has touched your mind and allows you to touch others. Envision the energy being sent out like a stream of light in the shape of a cone. The apex of the cone is your third eye and the base reaches as far and wide as you need it to, encompassing all, enlightening all, and changing all with the radiant healing energy of crystal-directed love.
7. Finally, clear the crystals with water, sound, or smoke and return them to storage or display until you have need to call upon them again. You can also carry them with you when you are called to direct action so that you may stay grounded and protected, loving and aware. If you are called to keep them with you, you may skip the clearing step until you are ready to rededicate them to another purpose.

Crystal Messages

During the Victorian era, it was common for a love relationship to be acknowledged with a "regard" ring. A regard ring was a token of high esteem that would serve as a promise for an engagement. The word "regard" was symbolized by ruby, emerald, garnet, and diamond. Think about playful messages you could spell with crystals in order to modernize and make magick with this charming tradition.

Chapter 7

CRYSTALS and BEAUTY

While crystals can be used to soothe your emotions, heal and cleanse your aura, and impart vitality to your etheric body, crystals can also have a beneficial effect on your corporeal body. Far from being just a form of glamour magick, which is sometimes used to conceal or transform, crystal magick can interact with your physical appearance to put you in touch with your core. Whether there is a persona or vibe you want to project, a desire you wish to signal, or a specific alignment with self-acceptance that you need to integrate, using crystals will help you achieve all of these and more. In this chapter, you will learn how to use crystal slices and slabs to charge your personal care products. You will understand how using crystals can make simple beauty routines into magickal rituals to inspire confidence. With information on selecting appropriate crystals to wear for different purposes, you can build a collection of beads, points, and pendants with intention, confidence, and purpose. You will also learn how to use crystals on specific parts of your body in order to achieve a desired result. Whether you are choosing crystal jewelry for fashion or a pendant for heart opening, this chapter will help you make the choices that will benefit you the most from head to toe.

CRYSTAL VISAGE

While there is no doubt that crystals can add beauty to your environment, they can also be used to enhance your appearance. Crystal face rollers are popular and there is an interesting reason why. Usually made of jade or rose quartz, these simple beauty tools feature a crystal polished into a tapered cylinder that is threaded through with a wire attached to a small handle. The crystal is gently moved across the face in an upward motion, which accomplishes a few things. First, the gentle pressure is stimulating to the fascia, which is a type of tissue that surrounds all the muscles of the body. The fascia is very thin, and the act of rolling a crystal gently over the face creates a fluid exchange, similar to wringing out a sponge that can then be rehydrated and refreshed. Additionally, the gentle pressure and the stimulating effect it has can relax the facial muscles and improve the appearance of the overlying skin tissue. Because the skin is delicate and the fascia is beneath the skin, it is very important to use a very gentle touch. And finally, because crystals are used to conduct energy, you can imbue your crystal roller with an intention and then transfer that intention into your appearance. This can easily be turned into a meditative practice as a regular part of self-care by focusing on the energy you wish to project to the world. You can close your eyes and repeat affirmations to yourself while you delicately use your crystal roller. For example, while rolling across your forehead, bring yourself into a quiet and calm state of mind and engage with your third eye and focus on the affirmation:

My mind is clear.
I have no fear.
My third eye is open and bright.
I awaken my psychic sight.
May my desires be known to me.
May I embrace all that I see.

Continue using the crystal roller across your cheeks, starting at your jawline and moving upward, then from the side of your nose out toward your ears. As you roll, envision the energy transfer taking place and use this time to implement your own happiness with an affirmation:

Blessed be my smile.
May it enchant all that I see.
Blessed be my style.

May I show the very best of me.
Blessed be my joyful heart.
My laughter is always heard.
Blessed be my sacred art
And blessed be my word.

You can also use a crystal roller on your neck to activate your throat chakra and improve communication. Think about the types of communication you need to accomplish, and as you use the roller starting at the base of your neck, moving upward, envision that miscommunications are removed from your reality. Cultivate clarity by formulating direct affirmations such as:

My voice is empowered.
I only speak truth.
My voice is respected.
I am clearly understood.
My voice is heard.

When you complete your affirmations and light-touch crystal rolling, you can finish your mindful self-care with a crystal-infused face mist. This is easily accomplished by adding a crystal to your favorite face mist or by making your own. The good thing about making your own face mist is that you can create it with a specific intention in mind and use it whenever you need to conjure up that particular state of being.

If you don't have a crystal face roller and you are not interested in getting one, you can still achieve similar results by using a small crystal sphere. Choose a small crystal sphere, around ¾ inch in diameter, and using an extremely light touch, gently roll it over your face in a slow upward motion starting at your jawline, up to your temple, to the center of your forehead, then repeat on the other side of your face. If you aren't sure which crystal to use, consult the crystal library in Part 2. Do you need to calm down? Choose a grounding crystal such as jade. Are you interested in augmenting and projecting your spiritual nature? Use an amethyst ball. And if you just need a little clarity, a clear quartz ball will work just fine.

These are the crystals used most often in spells for beauty:

- Amazonite
- Amethyst
- Jade
- Moonstone
- Rose quartz
- Selenite
- Sunstone

CRYSTALS AND TRADITIONAL EAST ASIAN MEDICINE

Crystals can be used for healing as well as beauty. One ancient method of crystal beauty and healing that is enjoying a modern moment is the traditional practice of gua sha. Gua sha has been a part of Traditional Chinese Medicine for thousands of years although many people are discovering its positive effects anew. Of course, it is highly recommended that any treatments be rendered by an experienced and knowledgeable clinician with proper training in order to minimize risks. And while crystal treatments are not a substitute for modern medicine, their practice has endured because they work for so many people. Gua sha addresses the issue of stagnancy by stimulating circulation. Using a crystal scraper, usually made of jade, amethyst, or rose quartz, you can improve your appearance and reduce stress by targeting parts of your face. A gua sha scraper is ergonomic in that it is flat and comfortable to hold, with a tapered edge that is moved around the jaw, behind the ears, across the cheeks, and other key points of the body such as the neck and throat. Be very careful because a common side effect of gua sha is petechiae, spots that cause a reddening of the skin. This reddening can persist, so it is necessary to plan for healing or downtime to give the petechiae time to resolve, around two to three days, after which your skin will appear smoother and brighter.

CRYSTAL BEAUTY SPELL

To incorporate crystals into your beauty routine, you will need a few simple, easy-to-obtain objects. Regardless of your gender identity, there are times when witches want to look their best. While appearances are not paramount, there is a connection between how you look and how you feel. A crystal will not change your appearance unless you are physically wearing it, but a crystal can also be a powerful link between your confidence, how you present yourself, and how you feel about your appearance. Using crystals in your beauty routine is a way to take back your power and open a gateway to self-acceptance and increase your confidence.

Crystal Beauty Spell

You Will Need

- Tapered candle or medium spell candle
- Stick of incense
- Incense holder
- Rose quartz crystal slab (or a geode slice, natural or dyed in your favorite color)
- Shallow glass of water
- Washcloth or linen napkin
- Product that you frequently use, such as a perfume or cologne, a cosmetic, or a topical such as a moisturizer

Directions

1. Assemble your ingredients at a time when you can dedicate some solitude and focus on how you feel about yourself. Light the candle and get in a comfortable position with your objects within easy reach. Focus on the candle flame as you envision yourself as powerful and pleasing to the eye.
2. Next, light the stick of incense and place it in the holder. Allow the scent to rise and greet you. Center yourself in the feeling of not only being visually pleasing but also having warmth in your heart, full of self-acceptance, and having a pleasing scent as well.
3. Take your crystal slab or geode slice and hold it in front of your eye with the candle a safe distance behind it. See how the light of the flame permeates and enlivens the colors and the inclusions in your crystal.
4. Hold the slab or slice high over the burning incense so the smoke wafts around it. Notice how the smoke will gather and travel across the surface. Turn the crystal over to get a nice smoke bath on both sides.
5. Place the crystal in the water and turn it over three times. As you turn the crystal, speak the following charm:

   Beauty born of earth
   Inherent in its worth
   Your lovely scent does rise
   Charming to the eyes.
   As the fire gently burns
   In the water you will turn
   Fire, water, earth, and air
   Behold your beauty everywhere.

6. Remove the crystal from the water and gently dry it with the cloth. Place your beauty product of choice on top of the crystal and repeat the charm with a twist:

   I am born of earth
   Inherent in my worth.
   The fires of my spirit burn.
   Waters of wisdom turn and turn.
   By the fire, water, earth, and air
   My beauty radiates everywhere.

7. Envision the power and magick of the crystal transferring into your chosen product. When you feel that the energy transfer has occurred, apply the product to your face and body as you normally would. Bask in your renewed confidence. Allow the candle to burn down. If you cannot attend to the candle, put it in a safe place such as the center of an empty bathtub.

How to Discern an Energy Transfer

Crystals are conductors. It is in their nature to carry energy in many forms, from heat to electricity to intentions. An energy transfer may be observable. You might notice a sudden flicker of the candle flame or that your incense smoke seems to dance. Observe the reactions in your surrounding environment and check these manifestations of change against your intuition. Sometimes a transfer is deeply felt even when it cannot be outwardly observed.

CRYSTAL MIST

When you need a quick boost to your spirits, a crystal face mist is an excellent way to refresh your face and perk up your energy. This simple recipe is easy to prepare in small batches and can be used for a variety of purposes in addition to refreshing your face. The four variations in the following table will give you options to explore. Choose the one that resonates with you the most strongly and then try another. You can also experiment by creating your own blends that are suited to your identity and needs.

Crystal-Infused Face Mist Basic Instructions

You Will Need

- 4 ounces purified water
- 1–2 drops essential oil of your choice
- ¼ teaspoon aloe vera gel
- 4-ounce cobalt spray mist bottle
- Small crystal chips

Directions

1. Combine the water, essential oil, and aloe in the bottle. Shake vigorously, then add the crystal chips.
2. Allow the water to settle and use it when you need to heighten, change, or subdue your energy or whenever you are in need of a refreshing pick-me-up.

Customized Crystal Mist

Repeat the previous steps and customize your bottle to suit your needs by pairing specific crystal chips with carefully chosen oils in order to get the result you want. Consult the following table to customize your crystal face mist:

Crystal Mist Customization Table

Desire	Crystal	Essential Oil
Stimulating	Carnelian	Peppermint
Calming	Amethyst	Lavender
Love	Rose quartz	Rose
Healing	Aventurine	Bergamot

CRYSTAL PENDANTS AND BEADS

Adornment is one of the earliest ways that people began working with crystals. The attraction, the power, and the allure of crystals gave birth to trade routes and entire industries. In modern times, the fascination with crystals has only grown, and wearing crystals in the form of jewelry, talismans, and charm bags is as popular as ever. Thinking about how and where you place crystals on your body is magickal when you do it with intention. Crystals can be worn in a variety of ways. Wearing crystals with intention can elevate the experience of accessorizing. Choosing color with intention is a form of magick in itself, but certain crystal pairings can lend another layer of confidence, an additional way to express yourself magickally and achieve your desired outcome. When you put a crystal on your body, whether it is against your skin or over your clothes, you are taking action. Any action that you take with intention, with mindfulness, and in a ritualized way becomes a spell. Add a spoken charm and the effect is even more potent. And when you combine crystals with your attire, you are literally wearing your intention. It is a method of speaking, of showing the universe that you are continually taking action toward manifesting. Here are some suggestions for crystal jewelry that you may consider.

Manifesting Magick with Crystal Beads

Anything worn around the neck or near the heart has an impact on communication ability, how you are perceived and understood, and how you feel. Matters of the heart can be influenced in a positive way by wearing crystals.

- To strengthen a committed relationship, wear a strand of rose quartz beads and layer them with a strand of peridot. Peridot is a relationship healer, and rose quartz encourages loving vibrations.
- To improve confidence in matters of importance, wear a short strand of lapis lazuli and an amethyst pendant. The deep blue will amplify your throat chakra, making it possible to communicate with authority, while the amethyst will elevate your energy so that you are more commanding when you need to be.

- To anticipate an augmentation of wealth, mix amber or citrine with aventurine or prasiolite. The gold tones resonate with the color of the sun, the energy source, the life giver, and the green stimulates growth. Green is also a common color for currency.

THE BEST CRYSTALS FOR RINGS

Rings are highly charged talismans that symbolize many things: committed relationships, unity, and power. Rings are given as tokens of love and friendship. They can also represent a promise. One of the most important things to consider when choosing a crystal for a ring is the relative hardness of the crystal. In gemological terms, hardness simply means resistance to scratching. Crystals with a hardness of seven or above on the Mohs scale will be durable enough to wear in a ring. Anything less than a seven will be prone to chips and breaks. This can be upsetting if you have charged the crystal to be a working magickal tool. Choosing crystals with a higher hardness rating will last longer and withstand the knocks and blows of daily activities.

In addition to hardness, you will want to think of the auspicious attributes and magickal associations of your hands. The left hand is generally associated with feminine energy. Crystals worn on the left hand can represent things that you wish to receive. The right hand is associated with masculine energy, so choose crystals that represent the things that you wish to give energy to. Even certain fingers have magickal correspondences. Use the following chart to learn more about the magickal correspondences of the fingers and which crystals can harmonize with the energy that they represent:

Crystals and Correspondences for Rings

Thumb	Forefinger	Middle finger	Ring finger	Pinkie finger
Venus	Jupiter	Saturn	Sun	Mercury
Emerald, clear quartz, jade	Lapis lazuli, azurite, amethyst	Onyx, obsidian, garnet	Citrine, amber, ruby	Moonstone, aquamarine, peridot

CRYSTALS FOR YOUR WRISTS

Crystal beads on an elastic band can be easily found in a variety of mineral types and sizes. A bracelet with small to medium crystal beads will have anywhere from thirty to forty individual beads, which can be used for mindfulness as well as manifesting. For example, if you wish to do a releasing spell in order to break a negative thought pattern or a negative habit, wear an onyx bracelet, and every time you catch yourself faltering and engaging in negative self-talk or tempted to indulge in a habit you wish to break, move the bracelet to your other wrist. The black beads will help absorb negativity, and moving the bracelet from one wrist to another will give you a replacement action to take instead of strengthening the pattern you wish to change. You can also choose crystals for each wrist that represent what it is you want to receive and what you would like to release.

CRYSTAL BEAUTY BLESSING BOWL

Creating a blessing bowl is a way to accomplish two things: invoking the state of being that you wish to call in and giving thanks and gratitude for blessings received. This is a powerful form of sympathetic magick because the construct of the bowl is the vessel that holds your intention, and through the act of creating it, you are already acting in accord. Furthermore, it functions as a beautiful piece of sympathetic magick in that you are giving thanks for the blessings that have already been received. You are putting yourself in the receptive state and aligning your energy with the thought that the manifestation you are seeking has already come to pass.

Creating a Crystal Beauty Blessing Bowl

A blessing bowl for beauty can assuage feelings of insecurity and act as a counterbalance to low self-esteem. It is a confidence-boosting exercise in self-acceptance and celebration to bring out your beauty through a blessing bowl.

You Will Need

- Votive candle
- Glass bowl
- Coarse sea salt
- 4 small crystal clusters
- 12–20 tumbled or rough small crystals
- 1 tablespoon crystal chips
- 8 bay leaves
- Fine-point felt-tip pen

Directions

1. Light the candle and place it in the center of the bowl. Surround the candle with the salt.
2. Place the four small clusters in between the candle and the sides of the bowl in the north, east, south, and west quadrants.
3. Arrange the tumbled or rough crystals in between the quadrants.
4. Add the chips on top of the tumbled or rough crystals.
5. Take the bay leaves and write upon them the things you like the most about yourself. Some examples:
    - Your greatest achievement
    - Your greatest love
    - Your strongest passion
    - Your source of power
    - Your favorite activity
    - Your highest hope
    - Your favorite scent
    - Your favorite song
    - Your proudest moment
6. Once you have written on the leaves, you will read those things aloud to yourself and experience all the parts of you that bring joy and pleasure and radiate beauty and happiness into the world.
7. Tuck the bay leaves in between the crystals so that they are standing up.
8. Enjoy the candlelight and embrace the beauty that naturally flows forth from you. Allow the candle to burn down. If you cannot attend to your spell candle, place it somewhere safe such as in the middle of an empty bathtub.

CRYSTAL CLEAR BEAUTIFUL COMMUNICATION SPELL

Clear communication is sexy. Being able to articulate your needs and being open to listening to others is a solid way to invoke beauty because being honest and clear and feeling understood is highly attractive.

Crystal Clear Beautiful Communication Spell

You Will Need

- Your preferred communication device: cell phone, tablet, or pen and paper
- Azurite
- Lapis lazuli
- Blue sapphire
- Small charm bag that can fit the crystals

Directions

1. Put your communication device in front of you. Take the three crystals and touch them first to your throat and then to your third eye, one at a time. Then place them on your device and recite the charm:

   My third eye is open.
   My needs are clear.
   My voice is strong.
   I have nothing to fear.
   Beauty attends me
   Ever at my side.
   I listen, I hear,
   I trust and confide.

2. Now you are open and secure to make a beautiful path of communication into your life. Place the three crystals in a charm bag and keep them next to your phone or the other device that you chose.

CRYSTAL BEAUTY JAR SPELL

A simple crystal jar spell to infuse your personal care routines with magick is a wonderful way to boost your confidence, and confidence is widely held to be an attractive trait. Using a combination of goddess energy with the power of the full moon, this crystal spell will give your beauty routine extra magick.

Crystal Beauty Jar Spell

The apatite in this spell is a revealer that will assist in your beauty being projected outward. The aquamarine and rose quartz harmonize with the goddess of love, Aphrodite, who was renowned for her beauty. Amazonite also functions as a revealer and will connect the properties of the crystals with the products they are touching through the law of contact. The crystals you use in this spell can be a combination of tumbled stones, points, and chips.

You Will Need

- Your favorite beauty products: for example, a special lipstick, moisturizer, and so on
- Large, clean glass jar (about 32 ounces) with a lid
- Aquamarine
- Amazonite
- Apatite
- Rose quartz

Directions

1. Place the beauty products (still in their containers) in the jar.
2. Add the crystals to the jar so that they are around and on top of your beauty products.
3. If you like, you may recite the charm as you place the crystals on and around the products:

   Beauty revealed.
   Beauty is healed.
   Beauty, I feel.
   Beauty is sealed.

4. Leave the jar open on your windowsill on a full moon night, or leave it out of doors if that is available to you.
5. Then, once the night has passed and the moon in her luminous beauty has infused your intention, close the lid on the jar.
6. Remove the products whenever you wish to use them and feel the extra glow of moonlight and crystal magick on your body and face.

THE BEAUTY OF CRYSTAL BEADS MANIFESTATION SPELL

You can elevate any bracelet or necklace of crystal beads into a magickal talisman by realizing the pure potential of the power you are holding. A circle of beads is a closed circuit that energy can freely flow through in order to enact a transformation.

The Beauty of Crystal Beads Manifestation Spell

For this spell, you will be using a crystal bead strand whose number of beads can be divided by thirteen. This can be either a bracelet or a necklace. The beads must be drilled through and preferably round. The type of crystal bead should be one that aligns with the energy or situation you need to manifest. The beads should not have a clasp but should be strung in a complete circle either on elastic, silk, or cord.

You Will Need

- **Crystal bead strand that can be divided in increments of 13**

Directions

1. Choose any bead as a starting point. It doesn't matter which one because it will be part of an unbroken circle.
2. You will touch and spin this first bead between your fingers, pulling at it gently so that you can see the drill hole.
3. You will perceive this hole as an opening in the field in your reality. This is the place that your manifestation will channel through. As you spin the bead, recite the charm:

I call to me
The object of my need
Pass through to me
I am open to receive.

4. Each individual bead will be a step on the pathway to actualizing your objective. Your first visualization is the big picture. Spin the bead and say:

   I imagine (this is the overarching goal that you will paint in your mind with broad strokes).

5. The second bead brings you to visualizing the details. Spin it in your fingers and say:

   I envision (this is the big picture with specific details about what manifesting it will feel like and how this will positively impact your life).

6. Spin the third bead and say:

   I open (here is where you make room for the manifestation to come into your life).

7. Spin the fourth bead between your fingertips and say:

   I determine (here you will start visualizing how you are going to manifest and what steps you need to take).

8. As you touch and spin the fifth bead, say:

   I invoke (this is your formal request spoken to your goddesses or gods, your ancestors, or your spirit guides).

9. Spin the sixth bead and say:

   I channel (here you engage with the opening and get in a receptive state).

10. Spin the seventh bead and say:

    I receive (you are opening yourself to become one with the channel).

11. Spin the eighth bead and say:

    I allow (give yourself permission to take in the bounty that you are claiming; get out of your own way).

12. Spin the ninth bead and say:

> *I examine (here is where you will take ownership of your desires; be honest with yourself about accepting what is flowing to you).*

13. Spin the tenth bead and say:

> *I transform (this gives you the opportunity to address any blocks that are coming up after you examine the situation).*

14. Spin the eleventh bead and say:

> *I integrate (here is where you will become one and the same with your desire, which has to manifest because you are now connected; you are bringing it through).*

15. Spin the twelfth bead and say:

> *I accept (revel in the delight that comes from knowing your dreams are coming true).*

16. Spin the last bead and say:

> *I know (this is your final task, to act in accord and in absolute certainty that you are in alignment in thought, word, and deed with your desired outcome).*

17. If you are wearing a necklace with more than thirteen beads, you may repeat the spell as you work each bead into a spin. It is important to touch them all and get that kinetic energy running through the entire strand. Wear the bracelet or necklace as a reminder to act in accord with your desired outcome.

Chapter 8

CRYSTALS for DIVINATION

The use of crystals in divination can be traced back to very ancient civilizations and is still practiced today. From onyx scrying mirrors to gemstone pendulums, crystals can be used to enhance your psychic powers because they are magickal tools that can aid your ability to see beyond the mundane. In this chapter, you will learn the fascinating history of how crystals were used for obtaining psychic visions, as well as some of the ancient practices from days of old and how these have been adapted for the modern age. You will find information on how to use crystals as sacred tools for trance, prophesying, conjuring, and more. From classic crystal ball gazing to obsidian glass scrying as well as spells for calling in spirits to communicate through crystal pendulums, you will learn how to interact with certain carved crystals in a deeply magickal way.

SCRYING: CRYSTAL DIVINATION

Scrying is an occult art by which a magick practitioner uses a reflective surface as a tool to set off a chain of physical and metaphysical occurrences that give the witch a glimpse into a world otherwise inaccessible or unseen. Scrying is believed to be many different things. Some people have regarded it as an art, a practice that can be developed and honed. Others have described it as a gift; some people possess this ability of seeing beyond, while others do not. And some people believe it to be a combination of the two. For example, if you possess the ability and you also develop your practice, then scrying is something you are going to be able to do successfully. If you do not possess the ability, you can develop it by practicing.

Think of it as you would any other pursuit. Take, for example, activities that require physical and mental stamina. Scrying isn't all that different. Suppose you wanted to be a professional athlete, such as a gymnast, or an artist such as a dancer. You would spend a lot of time practicing skills from an early age if you wanted to take your pursuit to a high level. You would have to develop a growth mindset and recover from losses, failures, and disappointments. The important thing is to keep going. You might not make it to the big leagues or to the Olympics, but winning a pickup game or turning a decent cartwheel is a worthwhile endeavor if it brings you happiness and pleasure. Set realistic goals for yourself and learn from the process.

These are the crystals used most often in spells for scrying and divination and revealing:

- Amazonite
- Apatite
- Apophyllite
- Beryl
- Clear quartz
- Charoite
- Emerald
- Labradorite
- Malachite
- Obsidian
- Onyx
- Topaz
- Unakite

Basics of Scrying

A lot of scrying is done with crystals, including obsidian, onyx, beryl, and clear quartz. Scrying can be accomplished with basically any reflective material. Metal can work, as can water and even ink. The key attribute is the reflective nature of the surface, and many crystals are ideally suited to be scrying tools because their surfaces can be polished to a smooth and highly reflective degree. Using crystals for scrying is highly recommended. In fact, they are perfect tools for the modern witch because they are natural, obtainable, and beautiful. There is no better way to determine if you have an aptitude for scrying than to try it out.

Much like tarot cards or runes, scrying is a method of divination where a witch can cast about for a query either for themself or for another person. Even though scrying is not a particularly easy occult pursuit, most of the difficulties are surmountable if you are dedicated to it. The prerequisites are an abundance of patience, dedicated chunks of time, and a quiet place where a witch can work undisturbed. These are not always possible to come by in our modern age; however, this shouldn't deter you. If you have the talent for scrying, it will be easier and faster to unlock your gift than you think it will be, so you might as well try. And if you possess an ancient hidden power, wouldn't you want to know?

In scrying, you are basically focusing your eyes to the point where your optic nerves get so tired that they stop working. If you are curious how long this first step takes, test it out by staring at a windowpane. Eventually, your brain gets a little tired of the fact that you have chosen to stare at a windowpane, and it tells your optic nerves to stop sending it that particular kind of information. So then what you perceive is that as you are staring at the windowpane, the panes start to disappear. Your optic nerves stop sending that particular image to your brain so that to your eye, the panes seem to disappear. When you scry, you are persisting in tiring the optic nerves so that the "outside to in" images stop being transmitted, allowing the brain to engage in a new way.

Since the optic nerves have stopped sending the image, the brain will fill in the space that was left empty once the eye stopped transmitting. The brain then has the chance to send an "inside to out" image that is then projected onto the surface of the crystal, creating a visual representation of thought. Now comes the magickal part. Instead of just allowing the brain to create any random thought and throw it onto the blank canvas of the crystal surface, you treat this activity as a sacred meditation. You cultivate the trancelike state of meditation before you even start scrying to make sure you are not distracted or preoccupied so that you don't just project your subconscious fears or stream-of-consciousness, inconsequential mental banter onto your crystal. Prepare yourself for a true vision, put in the time and the work, and you just might get something really magickal.

CRYSTAL BALL GAZING

There are few witch's tools more iconic than the crystal ball. The image of the fortune teller conjuring the unknown before a clear globe is as ubiquitous as a witch on her broom. And while crystal balls remain a popular method of divination, they are, in fact, quite ancient. Crystal balls have been associated with power for a very long time. The Orphic poem "Lithica" describes an object called "siderites" or "ophites," which was a heavy black magick sphere. As a testament to the sacred nature of the crystal ball, it was ritually cared for. The ball was clothed and tended to. Sacrifices would be offered to it. People believed that caring for the sphere in this manner, as though it were sacred and alive, meant that a soul could inhabit it. Similarly, the Zoroastrians would ritualize the use of a "golden ball" for magickal purposes. The ball was carved with symbols and held with leather straps that were swung around and around. The mage, or diviner, would focus on the moving sphere until they fell into a trance. Only then would they receive psychic visions.

Crystal Ball Caution

Crystal balls are powerful at bending and focusing light. When your crystal ball is not in use, never leave it exposed to direct sunlight. Always keep it away from light or draped with a dark cloth. As a concave lens, a crystal ball is capable of pinpointing a ray of light such that it may start a fire.

So what is it, exactly, that the witch is conjuring in the crystal? The answer to that question lies entirely in the witch's intention and ability to interact with spirit. Queries are sent. Visions are received. Communication ensues. Information is transferred and understanding takes place. A typical breakdown of crystal ball scrying goes (or can go) something like this:

- **The witch prepares.** This preparation is going to look different for everyone. It might begin with a ritual bath or the setting up of an altar. It could look like a combination of physical and spiritual cleansing such as a sacred water asperge or a smoke clearing. Whichever method you use to enter sacred space should be done with meticulous attention to detail. No witch wants to be half entranced only to be jolted back to the mundane plane by external interference. Plan and prepare and move accordingly.

- **The witch protects.** Now is the time to raise your psychic shields. Yes, you want to conjure the crystal and receive a spiritual download, but discarnate spirits are not automatically benevolent. Hang a broom on the door. Place bells on the doorknobs. Hang a horseshoe above entryways. Place mirrors on the windowsills. Whatever form of protective magick that is effective and relevant to your practice, enact it before you go into a trance state.
- **The witch illuminates.** You will need some kind of light source. It is the light that reflects off of the surface of the polished crystal that gives you the focal point to center your attention. Set up your candles so that you have a play of light between the source and the surface.
- **Focus on the light.** The points of light reflecting off of the crystal are going to tire out your optic nerves if you focus on them long enough.
- **The trance is invoked.** If you use a mantra, start repeating it now. If you practice meditative breathing, engage those skills. Whatever method you use for trance, once you have begun to focus on the light, this is the time to release your own thoughts, truly clear your mind, let go, and get ready to observe the changes at hand.
- **The mind opens.** With your eyes tired out and your mind clear, your brain has time to behave in a new way. At first you might not see anything different at all. Or the entire ball might disappear. Most people describe a phenomenon of mist.
- **The mist gathers.** The mist is a result of the interrupted transmission from the eyes. At this point, instead of seeing with your eyes, you are seeing with your soul. Relax into the vision and start accepting what you are being shown. The mist is widely believed to be the spirit entering the crystal, and this is your gateway, your point of contact into the unseen world.
- **The witch receives.** Now you are able to take in the vision. Crystal ball gazing is similar to channeling but in a different modality. Some people are better with words, while some are more adept at understanding images. Whatever your natural aptitudes are, allow them to shine right now. Give yourself permission to accept and to interpret. Write down your visions in your grimoire to see if they are significant and hold meaning when you are not under a trance. Practice and you will get better at it, just like with anything else.

- **The witch returns.** Modern witches often refer to a spiritual encounter with the oracle as a "download." Once you stop receiving information in the form of images and symbols, this is a signal to do some grounding and slowly allow yourself to enter back into the mundane world, leaving the liminal plane. You can do this by touching the ground or floor, giving thanks for visions and wisdom received, breathing deeply into your knowledge, and letting your conscious mind once again balance your subconscious mind so that you can "code switch" back to a place that is no longer between worlds.

USING A CRYSTAL SCRYING MIRROR

Witches use more than crystal balls for scrying. Technically, any reflective surface will suffice, but there are several appropriate choices from the crystal world to consider. Scrying mirrors are typically black. A flat black polished circle of obsidian or onyx makes for a very powerful scrying mirror. Like with all crystal carvings, the price will depend on the size and quality of the crystal. A scrying mirror does not need to be large in order to work, but it does need to be consecrated. The "magick mirror" of faerie tales provides information because it is inhabited by a spirit, and in modern witchcraft, there are definite parallels to this idea. If you are not a spiritual witch and do not work with spirits or deities, you are going to have a different experience with scrying. Some witches have deep spiritual connections and deeply held spiritual beliefs. When a practice of magick is centered on spirit, it makes scrying somewhat easier because the relationship to the spirit world is already there. If you are already working with spirits or deities, you should use the gods of your understanding in your scrying work. If you are not a spiritual witch, you may find success by tapping into natural magick and calling upon the mighty earth energies. Be assured that the earth has seen all, experienced all, and accepted and released all. The earth is a powerful energy to invoke through a crystal, and you may find that you are able to access what you seek in this manner.

The steps are similar to crystal ball scrying, but you will have to make some adjustments due to the nature of the tool. For example, if you do not have a stand for your scrying mirror, you will find yourself leaning over it for an extended period of time. This can lead to physical discomfort that is going to distract you from your spell.

First, find a comfortable way to interact with your mirror. If you are seated, have the mirror propped up in as vertical a position as its stand will allow. If your mirror does not have a stand, you can try propping it up between two crystals, one in the front and one in the back, provided that the mirror is small, no more than 2–3 inches in diameter. Larger mirrors will be too heavy (and too expensive) to risk being balanced in such a manner. Another option is to place a sliced geode behind the mirror with another crystal in front of it to keep it from slipping forward. Make sure that it is at eye level before you begin. If you are comfortable standing for medium-to-long periods of time, consider hanging the mirror on your wall.

SCRYING SPELL OF THE FOUR CHARMS

In this spell, you will scry in a mirror and receive insight into a question or situation relating to your immediate need. Be prepared to receive symbolic visions. Following the spell is a reference table to help you interpret your psychic vision. For your scrying mirror, onyx, obsidian, or jet is preferred, but if these are not available, a dark blue crystal may suffice. While there are plenty of dark blue crystals that hold a polish extremely well and have a lustrous surface, black is the preferred color. The size is unimportant.

Scrying Spell of the Four Charms

You Will Need

- Tapered candle
- Stick of incense
- Charged water, such as moon water or tap water infused with a few drops of collected water such as rain, ocean, river, or melted snow
- Bowl of water large enough to accommodate the crystal mirror
- Crystal scrying mirror, as dark as possible
- Stand for the mirror (or a system for hanging it on a wall so that it remains vertically upright without your having to hold it)
- Your grimoire
- This book for aid in interpreting your vision

Directions

1. Create an environment where you can focus. Your goal is to create a structured inquiry grounded within a ritual so that you may gain insight into a situation, question, life event, or decision. Light the candle and incense and pour the charged water into a bowl. Take some deep breaths and make a conscious decision to engage with your intuition, rely on sensations, and will yourself into a receptive state by being open, energized, alert, relaxed, and trusting.
2. Hold the mirror as you formulate your query in your mind. This establishes the physical contact that becomes a link to the metaphysical.
3. When your question is clear, hold the crystal scrying mirror in front of your mouth and speak your query aloud so that the mirror is in contact with the vibration of your voice.
4. Clear the mirror with smoke from the incense and recite the first charm:

   Smoke and spirit, element of air
   Enter the mirror, and meet with me there.

5. Dip the mirror into the bowl of charged water and recite the second charm:

   Spirit of water, from the darkness and depths
   Reveal in the mirror the secrets you've kept.

6. Pass the mirror quickly through the candle's flame (on both sides) and recite the charm:

   Spirit of fire, burning and bright
   Enter the mirror and grant me your sight.

7. Place the scrying mirror on your altar or on the wall and recite the final charm:

   Spirits of earth, revealed through the land
   Show to me now the answer at hand.

8. Focus on the candlelight and the reflections in the mirror. Keep your mind focused on what you see, not on what you wish to see.
9. Once you begin to see images or symbols, engage in a dialogue with them. For example, if you see a heart, acknowledge what you see and ask it questions to gain information. The dialogue might go like this:

   I see the heart.
   What does the heart need?

10. As you remain in liminal space, stay in touch with your intuition and see if the feelings associated with the image are positive, negative, or neutral. You may see another vision or symbol. Speak them aloud in order so that you can remember them. For example:

   I see the heart. What does the heart need?
   I see the key. The key guards a secret.
   I see the heart and the key. The key is the keeper of the secret of the heart.

11. Continue having a dialogue with the mirror until the visions no longer appear or until you cannot sustain the liminal any longer. Record what you have seen in your grimoire and use this book to reference common symbols and their meanings. Then decide how to interpret by determining which definitions fit the circumstance surrounding your query.
12. Blow out the candle, pour the water into the earth, and blow the ashes of the incense into the wind. Give thanks to the spirits for queries answered and insight gained. Wrap the mirror in black cloth and put it away until you have the need to call upon it again.

Common Symbols and Their Meanings

Symbol	Meaning
Diagonal lines	Departure
Multidirectional lines or "branches"	Transformation or change
Open circle	Unity
Circle with a dot	Wealth
Maze or circular lines	Returning
Vertical line	Masculine energy
Spiral	Feminine energy
Apple	Loss
Heart	Love
Key	Secret
Scythe	Death
Black circle	Shadow

When you interpret symbols, you are making a correlation between a visual representation and what your psyche associates with that visual. Symbol interpretation is more of an art than a science, and you will have to rely on your intuition in order to discern meaning. What is auspicious for one person might mean the opposite to another. Take colors, for example. Yellow is associated with the sun, but it is also used to signify cowardice. Blue is a color of tranquility. It also has an association with sadness. As you learn the general meanings associated with symbols you are likely to see, pay close attention to how those symbols make you feel. Your interpretation will be subject to your culture, your beliefs, and your environment. Like crystals, which have had numerous meanings attached to them across many centuries by many different cultures, divination and interpretation can be fluid, changing, and still correct. Images that you may see are the result of one sense stimulating another sense. Every image will have at least two meanings. One is the manifest meaning, which is what the symbol visually resembles. The other is the latent meaning, which is the hidden context that the symbol represents. Your psychic ability is the sense that will uncover the latent meaning that is connected to the manifest meaning.

In this way, through the images that the eye transmits and the brain interprets, the psychic witch can transform an ordinary reality into something deeper and more meaningful. Engaging with universal constructs, even if they are simple at first, will elevate the soul and allow you to connect with a transcendent reality. The crystal is both your key and your gateway into this other realm.

Auspicious Days for Scrying

Culmination cycles such as a new or full moon are best for divination scrying. Other auspicious days include Wednesdays and Saturdays, as mystic energy is amplified at these times due to their associations with Odin and Saturn.

DIVINATION WITH A CRYSTAL PENDULUM

Crystals are the perfect tool for pendulum divination because they have enough weight without being too heavy. The weight on a pendulum has one job: to maintain tension by reaching for the earth. The earth is attracting the crystal in the pendulum through gravity, and you are communicating with spirit by way of this tool through a quite literal connection. Typically a crystal pendulum may be single point, doubled terminated, tumbled, sphere, or cone. Pendulum weights are cut into all kinds of shapes. The one you choose to work with will be determined by the shape or silhouette you have the strongest affinity for.

Divining with a pendulum is also known as dowsing. Dowsing is a process of discovery. You are looking to uncover something unseen. Historically, dowsing was used to locate water, but with modern aqueducts, water treatments, plumbing, reservoirs, and irrigation systems, the art of divining to find sources of water has lost a lot of its importance in the more developed parts of the world. With the effect of climate change looming and droughts becoming longer and more severe, you might see a return of interest in dowsing for water, so it is probably worth practicing. Divining and dowsing both have the same essential purpose: to locate something. You might use a crystal pendulum to locate a lost object, to find something that has been stolen, or to uncover hidden information. Whatever your divination needs, you can use a crystal pendulum in the following way:

Divination with a Crystal Pendulum

You Will Need

- Crystal pendulum

Directions

1. Get in a comfortable position where you can maintain focus. Hold the line of the pendulum between your thumb and forefinger; put enough tension in your fingers that you can feel your pulse. Focus on the pulses as you align yourself with the pendulum.
2. Allow the pendulum to come to a point of stasis. When you reach the balance point of stillness, maintain it until you are ready to command.
3. Use your mind (without moving your hand) to encourage the pendulum to move. You can start by thinking something clear and simple in a single word such as "auspicious" or "favorable" or "positive" or any other synonym for "affirmative."
4. Watch the pendulum for movement. It will generally take one of four paths: You may see a side-to-side motion, you may see a

back-and-forth motion, you may see a circular motion, or you may see an oscillating motion.

5. Note the movement and what you are thinking of when the movement takes place. This is your first answer. For example, if you are focusing on the word "auspicious" or even a simple "yea" and the pendulum starts swinging back and forth, then you can interpret a back-and-forth swing to represent a yes or positive response to your question.
6. Allow the pendulum to come to a still point and then formulate another thought, such as "inauspicious" or "no." Watch again for subtle movements. Stay still until the movement becomes clear. This is your opposite response in relation to your first focusing thought.
7. Once you have two definitives, you can get a more varied response by either adding subtleties or nuances to your thoughts, such as "positive with conditions" or "change this," or asking questions about time, location, distance, or any other "where" or "when" questions. Notice and remember the specific changes in movement when you adjust your thoughts. Keep track of the changes and then you will establish the definitions of various motions, which will make the answers to your queries more specific. Once you have established a range of pendulum motions and you know what they mean, then you can begin posing actual questions that you want to know the answers to. There is nothing wrong with beginning with a simple positive or negative, but true responses that reveal fate or fortune are rarely simple. Allowing yourself time and space to develop comfort and understanding with complexity will make you a more adept diviner.

ELEMENTAL CRYSTAL DIVINATION SPELL

Divination has been practiced for centuries. When you engage with spirits or an oracle in order to seek hidden knowledge, you must always recognize your own fallibility as well as the fact that you are tapping into a realm that is largely unknown and therefore unpredictable and largely unverifiable against anything other than your own experience. Divination is more art than science. Free will can impact any chain of events, and just because you divine information about the future does not mean that it is certain to come to pass. The better and more responsible outlook is to consult an oracle with the understanding that you are seeking information on likely outcomes of events as they stand at that particular moment in time so that you can move accordingly and put your energy where it will serve you best in order to bring about your desires.

Typical questions for divination involve simple queries that you feel that you need help or direction navigating, or really big issues that are deep-rooted. Any query from "Should I buy these concert tickets?" to "Will I ever forgive my mother?" or "Is this a good day to plant my herbs?" can be illuminated by consulting an oracle. To use crystals as an oracle, you will develop your intuition to connect with the earth and the mysteries of spirit. By using your intuition, you are developing your psychic gifts instead of looking up a predetermined response, reading it verbatim, and trying to force it onto your situation. Crystal divination is much more subtle and fluid and can be more useful for this very reason.

Elemental Crystal Divination Spell

You Will Need

- 4 spell candles: red, yellow, blue, and green
- Stick of incense
- Incense holder
- Piece of white paper folded twice toward the center to create 3 sections
- Pen
- Red crystal such as carnelian, garnet, or wulfenite
- Green crystal such as malachite, aventurine, or prasiolite
- Yellow crystal such as citrine, golden feldspar, or heliodor
- Blue crystal such as sodalite, celestite, or apatite

Directions

1. Prepare yourself for magick by getting into a meditative state. Take some deep breaths. Set the candles upon your altar, light them, and light the incense stick in its holder.
2. Take the white paper and write one phrase in each section.
3. In the folded section closest to you, write "Before me." This will represent the aspect that requires your immediate attention. This is your "right now."
4. In the middle section, write "Within me." This represents the energy that will manifest next. This is your emotional need.

5. In the third and final section, the one that is farthest away from you, write "Beyond me." This represents the influence that will dominate the future outcome.
6. Hold the red crystal in your hands and breathe into it. This is your fire element. Close your eyes and dedicate this crystal to your passion. This can be your love, desire, sex, life force, or the thing that drives you. Place the crystal in front of you.
7. Take the green crystal in your hands and breathe into it. This crystal is your earth element, and it represents what grounds you, your home, your source of stability, your support network. Place it beside your fire crystal.
8. Take the yellow crystal in your hands and breathe into it. This is your crystal of air and it represents change. This is your state of flux, your creative energy, all the aspects of you that manifest outwardly, including your social, professional, or creative roles in the world. Place it next to the green crystal.
9. Take the blue crystal in your hands and breathe into it. This is your water element, the seat of your emotions. It can also represent your shadow, the parts of yourself that you cannot readily engage with. These are the depths and hidden places of your heart and soul.
10. Now, with the paper right in front of you, hold all the crystals in your hands at once with your palms together as though in prayer. Start generating energy by rubbing your hands together and allow your energy to transfer into the crystals. Get a good steady rhythm going and then drop all the crystals at once onto the paper. Now you are ready to start intuiting the results.
11. Look at the crystals in the first section of the paper. Notice their position. The one closest to you is the aspect in need of your immediate attention. This is what you should attend to first.
12. Look at the crystals in the middle section. This is your internal landscape, or the influences that are governing how you feel and respond to your query. Take note of the position of the crystals. Are any crystals touching each other? This could indicate two aspects that you need to work in tandem.
13. Look at the crystals that are farthest away from you. These are the aspects that will become prominent in the days to come. Use this method of divination to adjust your course of action, set priorities, and come into your power.

14. When you have received insight from your crystals and you feel clear on what your next steps should be, blow out the candles and act accordingly.

THE MODERN CRYSTALLOMANCY SPELL

Crystallomancy, or divination with crystals, has been around for centuries. It started during the Elizabethan era and continued through the late 1800s and is still useful today. Traditional crystallomancy is done with two people, so you will need a partner or a coven member to try this method of divination.

The Modern Crystallomancy Spell

You Will Need

- Working partner in magick
- Dark room
- Clear and colorless crystal sphere
- Round flat black polished crystal such as jet or obsidian
- Grimoire and pen

Directions

1. Before entering the room, confer with your partner and decide which roles you will each take in the crystallomancy. One of you will act as the conduit between spirits and the other will be the medium and scribe. You may allow the crystals to decide this by seeing if one of you has a strong draw or affinity with the crystal, while the other participant feels more ambivalent toward the sphere or feels more interested in the mirror. One of you will hold the crystal sphere, the symbol of light, and this person will be the medium and scribe. The other will hold the black crystal mirror, and this person will be the channel, or conduit.
2. Once roles are determined, take the crystals and the grimoire and pen and enter the room. All lights should be out.
3. You will sit facing each other. The conduit will hold the black mirror with four fingers in front and with thumbs behind. It is very important that all fingers are touching the mirror to create an energy

loop. The conduit allows energy including pulse and breath to pass from hand to mirror and into the other hand and through the body.

4. The medium will hold the crystal of light. This provides the counterbalance to the dark mirror and allows the channel to be balanced and messages to be received. The medium will hold the clear crystal while gazing into the black crystal and wait for messages to appear.
5. Colors, symbols, ideas, words, or phrases may start to appear. Whichever of you is the medium puts down the crystal and takes up the grimoire in order to write down the divine messages. This typically induces a state of euphoria or rhapsody, as divination is one of the highest psychic gifts, and accessing this power is both pleasurable and intense.
6. When the transmission of energy and messages is complete, you may both leave the room and share experiences, read the grimoire, and interpret according to your personal knowledge and intuition.

Chapter 9

CRYSTALS for SPIRITUAL WISDOM

Crystals add layers of power to the practice of witchcraft, and so do witch's tools that incorporate or are directly made from crystals. Since ancient civilizations began categorizing crystals, they have been associated with mystical powers. Even without knowing how or why, we have always assumed crystals to have energetic power. The concept of energy as a scientific term has a specific definition: the ability to do work. In witchcraft, witches raise, harness, manipulate, and project energy in order to accomplish a spell, or a kind of occult "work," and the successful spell is often referred to as a magickal working. As people grow in wisdom, science and mysticism seem to move closer together instead of farther apart. We now know that crystals actually do have the ability to conduct and amplify energy. They are used in technology and in witchcraft because they are effective in both. Witches use all kinds of tools in spellcraft and ritual, and crystals have an important role in modern witchcraft. In this chapter, you will learn which tools can be made of crystals. Many magickal and mind-altering tools will be explored, including the use and effect of crystal singing bowls, crystal wands, and crystal athames, and you'll learn which crystals can balance the aura and align the chakras.

ALTAR CRAFT: MAGICKAL TOOLS MADE FROM CRYSTALS

Crystals are often used for awakening the witch to higher powers, bolstering intelligence, and sharpening the mind and other senses. A witch creates an altar as a sacred space to perform spells and rituals. Very specific magickal tools that correspond with elements and cardinal directions are customary in certain lineages of witchcraft. Many of these sacred objects have been made of out of crystals. It is not necessary to have every type of magickal tool made out of crystal, but it is something worth considering, particularly if you already have a clairvoyant affinity for crystals. Owning and using witch's tools made from crystals lends an additional layer of magick because crystals have their own inherent power in addition to the power of the form that they have been carved into.

Crystal Singing Bowls

Crystal singing bowls are powerful magickal tools that can induce a deep meditative state, relieve stress, and even improve your physical health. Similar to Tibetan singing bowls, which operate on the same principle, crystal singing bowls are made of quartz, are often frosted, and sometimes are dyed auspicious colors or adorned with metaphysical or religious symbols. Singing bowls are made from taking quartz sand and heating it until it is molten and then pouring it into a mold. The frosted appearance of the bowls indicates that the quartz does not have additives such as lead. The bowls create a vibrational harmonic resonance when they are played. In order to play a crystal singing bowl, the practitioner gently taps the side of the bowl with a mallet, which produces a musical note. Another way that a singing bowl is played is by moving the mallet around the rim of the bowl in a circular motion until the bowl produces a tone. The practitioner can control the volume and duration of the tone through speed and pressure exerted on the rim. The vibration of the tone can be heard aurally and also felt physically.

Crystal singing bowls vary in size and are used in sets in order to achieve harmonizing tones that have a beneficial impact on the body and mind. A practitioner may even place a crystal singing bowl directly on a person's body in order for them to feel the vibrations intensely. The vibrations will also bounce off any surfaces in the room where they are being played, such as the floor (provided it is not covered by rugs or carpet) and the walls. This can create a chamber of sound that washes over everyone in the room. Called a "sound bath," the effect of experiencing harmonizing tones played at deliberate intervals for the purpose of healing is very intense and effective at clearing energy blocks, removing stress, and restoring energy.

Crystal Wands

Witches use wands to represent the element of air in natural magick. They are also used for invoking, casting circles, and directing energy. A wand is an essential tool, and a witch's wand might be tipped with a crystal point or have different crystals adhered to the shaft of the wand, or the entire wand itself might be made of a particular type of crystal. And because each crystal mineral type has its own distinct metaphysical properties, it is possible for a witch to choose a wand with a specific attribute that suits their craft. The wand is synonymous with a witch's will, so you will often see a rainbow of crystals representing chakras set into the wand in order to produce a tool that can align with the etheric body of the witch. On the witch's altar, the wand is placed in the eastern quadrant, representing the element of air.

Crystal Athame

The athame is used to delineate sacred space, to cast a circle in which a sacred ritual is enacted. A witch will use an athame, or double-sided blade, to perform this magickal task. The circle is considered a place in and out of time, and by stepping inside the circle, the witch enters a place known as between the worlds. Since the athame is a magickal tool and is not used for cutting physical objects, it can be made of crystal.

Selenite is a common crystal used for carved ceremonial blades. Selenite is an extremely soft crystal, which makes it very easy to carve but also quite fragile. When using a selenite blade, it is imperative that you use it only for casting a circle and for cutting people into or out of the circle. Some of the benefits of using a selenite blade for witchcraft is its beautiful appearance. Selenite exhibits otherworldly optical properties such as adularescence and chatoyancy, giving any tools made from this crystal an exceptionally magickal appearance. Obsidian, jasper, and quartz are also crystals that are used to fashion ceremonial magickal daggers. On a witch's altar, the athame is placed in the southern quadrant, representing the element of fire.

Crystal Chalice

A crystal goblet, carved from clear quartz, was found by archaeologists in Mexico. Water inclusions contained within the crystal allowed scientists to verify its authenticity and suggest that it was made during the post-classic Mixtec period in Oaxaca sometime around C.E. 900–1521. The chalice is an elemental magickal tool used in witchcraft representing water, the emotions, and the feminine principle. A chalice made of crystal will have additional symbolism that is drawn not only from its form and purpose, but also from the energy of the crystal that it is made from. A chalice of crystal might be carved from calcite, agate, soapstone, or onyx. On the altar, it is placed in the western quadrant.

ELEMENTAL MAGICK WITH CRYSTALS

If you are already using crystals in your witchcraft or if you have tools that are made of crystals, it is still helpful to know how to maximize their power when setting up your altar. A witch's altar is a physical representation of many different things. It can be the stage where the witch interacts with spirits or deities. It can be a working surface where charms are made, herbs are combined, and candles are lit with intention. It can also be aesthetic, created with purpose, and imbued with energy. Here is a simple elemental attunement that you can use to set your intentions, dedicate your altar, or serve as a focal point for a crystal meditation.

Elemental Magick with Crystals

You Will Need

- Clean, clear 32-ounce glass jar
- Water
- ¼ cup coarse sea salt (optional)
- Crystal tower that aligns with your intention
- Assortment of tumbled crystals or chips that call to you
- Tea light candle

Directions

1. Fill the jar ¾ full with water. Add the salt (if desired) to the bottom of the jar. The salt's presence is to unite the water element with the

earth element, but since you will also be adding crystals from the earth into the jar, this step is optional.

2. Place the tower into the water. The water level should rise but not yet approach the top of the jar.
3. Add the other smaller crystals, dropping them into the water around the base of the tower. As you place the crystals, you can state your intention or the events you wish to manifest. Cultivate mindfulness as you watch the crystals fall through the water.
4. Take the tea light out of its tin and light it.
5. Float the tea light on top of the water.
6. The fire is consuming oxygen from the air while floating on top of the water surrounding the salt and crystals. This elemental attunement allows you to use the crystals to aid your mindfulness exercises if you wish to gaze upon the harmonious union of elemental power or if you want to use the configuration as a spell to manifest outcomes. Allow the tea light to burn the entirety of the wick.

An Extra Boost

You can also add a few drops of essential oil to the water to give your spell a boost.

AURA CLEANSING WITH CRYSTALS

Auras are light projections that give clairvoyant readers a sense of what state of health their spirit may be in. Auras are believed to be the light projections of the soul, and some sensitive witches are able to see them. Different-colored auras can indicate different states of well-being: emotional, spiritual, and psychic. If you should intuit an imbalance in your aura, you can correct this by using crystals as sympathetic antidotes.

You can determine the state of your aura by practicing aura reading. This is done by sitting before a mirror with a white blank wall behind you. Focus on the area just beyond your corporeal body to see if you are able to perceive your light body. If your light body is not perceptible to you, you might want to try finding someone who can either see and interpret auras or even photograph them. Once you have determined the state of your aura, you can determine if it is "high" or "low." Highs and lows indicate the intensity, duration, and frequency of the light waves interpreted by the eye as color. The goal is to achieve a balance in your aura to bring about a state of peace, centeredness, and calm, if that is what you desire. One indication of a balanced aura would be more secondary and tertiary colors than primary colors. For example, someone with a predominantly red aura might be experiencing some kind of threat to their survival or an emotional trauma. In order to heal, you would choose a crystal that is opposite of the presenting color in your aura. The antidote to red would be green. Experimenting with keeping green crystals such as jade, green tourmaline, prasiolite, or aventurine would help address this. Try different combinations of crystals to address the different frequencies that your aura might be revealing.

Sometimes a purple aura will indicate a heightened spiritual experience. While this is not undesirable, it is not always convenient or expedient. If you are feeling out of control during this heightened experience, because spiritual awakenings can also awaken you to painful or unpleasant truths and leave you feeling vulnerable to the harsh realities of the world, you may want to balance your aura by using crystals. Yellow is the antidote to purple, so working with citrine, topaz, heliodor, and golden feldspar (also known as golden healer) can bring you back to center.

Aura Crystals

While "aura" crystals have grown in popularity, they do not get their myriad colors from any sort of aura. The coating of an aura crystal is usually a film of titanium, which is not natural to the crystal and may even be concealing flaws or characteristics that would lower the value of the stone. While aura crystals are pretty, this type of treatment and its optical effect does not occur in nature.

CHAKRA BALANCING WITH CRYSTALS

Chakras are considered energy centers of the body, almost like spiritual organs. Just as the corporeal body has different systems that work together to take in nutrients and expel waste, the etheric body also has organs that allow you to access and explore your spiritual nature. Each chakra operates as a portal that can open and close and has often been described as being very similar to the pupil of the eye: Dilation and miosis either allow light in or block it out in order to maintain balanced perception. Chakras work in a similar fashion, and as the organs of the spiritual body, they benefit from attention to their health. For example, someone with excessive energy in their sacral chakra might present with their sexuality overt at all times. This in itself is not a problem unless the person with excessive sacral chakra energy finds it to be problematic. Most of the problems arise not from the chakra imbalance itself, but from how people respond to it. Some presenting as highly sexualized may find that they are being treated as a sex object more than they would like. Instead of moderating their behavior for the comfort of others, they can balance their sacral chakra so that the energy is not coming into contact with people they do not want to be intimate with. Conversely, a person with a blocked sacral chakra may feel cut off from achieving intimacy, and opening this chakra can be a healthy and healing experience. In the following table, you will find a list of crystals that are associated with seven chakras that all people are considered to be able to access with ease. You can use a crystal pendulum to determine if your chakra is blocked or is exhibiting excessive energy and then use the crystals from the table to either open that chakra if it is blocked or balance it with a color-opposite crystal. Many times you will not need to divine this information at all. As you grow in your connection to your etheric body, you will be able to tell through your thoughts, emotions, and choices where those blocks might be.

Crystal Chakra Correspondences

Crown Chakra (spiritual attainment and enlightenment)	Lapis lazuli, Sugilite
Third Eye Chakra (psychic awareness)	Amethyst, Clear quartz
Throat Chakra (communication, giving and receiving)	Sodalite, Azurite
Heart Chakra (love, giving and receiving)	Rose quartz, Jade
Solar Plexus Chakra (willpower)	Citrine, Turquoise
Sacral Chakra (sexuality)	Carnelian, Tiger's eye
Root Chakra (survival)	Garnet, Obsidian

CHARGING CRYSTALS

In Chapter 3, you learned various methods of clearing crystals of residual energy before using them for magick. In your spells and rituals, you will use crystals as receptacles, conductors, and directors of energy as well. In order to use a crystal, any type of crystal, in a magickal working such as a spell or ritual, you will want it to carry the energy of your intention so that it can be matched, amplified, and sent out into the universe in order to activate the desired result. After you have cleared your crystal, you can charge it through physical contact (touch), sound vibration (spoken words and charms), projection (thought), elemental contact (through use of magickal tools such as a wand, athame, chalice, and so on). Here are methods you may wish to employ in order to use your crystals for your spells and rituals:

- **Receiving energy:** During times of heightened energy, such as full moons and new moons, you can allow your crystals to receive energy by directly exposing them to moonlight, illuminating them with candlelight, or arranging them in a matrix arrangement on an inverted pentagram that indicates the invoking or receiving position.
- **Conducting energy:** Your crystals can be conduits of your intention through contact. After you charge your crystal, you can put it in direct contact with your magickal target. For example, if you are carving a jar candle for a spell, put the crystal at the base of the candle so it is touching. Or if you are using a tapered candle, you can bind the crystal directly to the candle. Another method is to place the crystal directly in the wax as the candle burns if the candle is large enough. This works well with candles that are in containers, but if the crystal is larger than half an inch or so, it can fall on the wick and put the candle out. Make sure that the crystal is far enough away from the wick so it doesn't extinguish the light.
- **Directing energy:** Arranging crystals in a matrix to bring about an alignment of events is a powerful method of manifestation. Some examples of matrices will be given in Chapter 11. You can also use crystals by holding them while you make invoking gestures as a way of directing energy. Crystals incorporated into your magickal tools will also direct energy. Be sure to inspect your tools and look for things like adhesives or glues that might actually be barriers to energy transfers. Adhesives and glues are convenient, but they prohibit direct contact and conductivity. Look for tools that are either made from crystals entirely or made with enough skill that the crystals are bound to the

tool by metal or cord or some other substance that does not come in between the crystal and the tool. For example, if you are using a wand tipped with crystal and the crystal is glued on, the glue is actually inhibiting the contact between the crystal and the wand, and it will not be as effective a tool as a crystal-tipped wand that is fitted and held in place with friction or metal.

CRYSTAL POWER PARTNERS

Some crystals work very well together to address and amplify a variety of states of being. The characteristics of particular crystals can be heightened when they are used in tandem with another crystal that has a similar purpose. Here you will find a reference table of different crystal companions that can accelerate and amplify desired emotional and spiritual states so that you can focus on your spells from a place of balance.

Crystal Power Pairs

Balance Sodalite and Rose quartz	**Banishing** Obsidian and Onyx	**Calming** Labradorite and Unakite
Channeling Moonstone and Clear quartz	**Clairvoyance** Selenite and Celestite	**Cleansing** Amethyst and Clear quartz
Communication Sodalite and Celestite	**Confidence** Obsidian and Rose quartz	**Courage** Bloodstone and Carnelian
Creativity Aventurine and Malachite	**Energy** Fluorite and Sunstone	**Friendship** Citrine and Rose quartz
Good Luck Amazonite and Pyrite	**Grounding** Hematite and Jasper	**Growth** Amethyst and Aventurine
Happiness Jade and Citrine	**Harmony** Lapis lazuli and Jasper	**Inner Peace** Aquamarine and Aventurine
Joy Sunstone and Citrine	**Love** Rose quartz and Rhodochrosite	**Road Opener** Unakite and Tiger's Eye
Stability Agate and Onyx	**Strength** Tiger's Eye and Ruby	**Truth** Sodalite and Lapis lazuli

No matter how you choose to use your crystals, whether it be for elemental magick, harmonizing your spiritual being, experiencing growth, or amplifying your magick, you will find crystals to be beautiful and resilient partners in magick. They will enhance your tools and imbue your witchcraft with sacred earth energy in a way that no other object can.

CRYSTAL-POWERED MANIFESTING GENERATOR SPELL

Use this spell when you need to motivate yourself to do difficult tasks or start the things that you may have been procrastinating on. You will use an assortment of crystals to open your solar plexus chakra and activate the sheer force of your will.

Crystal-Powered Manifesting Generator Spell

You Will Need

- Yellow candle
- Charoite
- Unakite
- Citrine
- Amber
- Book of Shadows
- Pen
- Small pouch, gold or yellow, 2 inches × 3 inches (optional)

Directions

1. Clear your space and clear your mind, and light the yellow candle. Focus only on the task at hand. This is the immediate obstacle that you are facing, the unattended issue or situation that you need to address. It could be work related, it could be something impacting your priority relationship, or it could be something you need to communicate but have been putting off because doing so would make you assume some kind of risk, emotional or otherwise. Let the mundane world fall away and let this issue take up a little space in your mind.
2. Put the four crystals in front of you. Arrange them in a crescent shape. This is the form of new beginnings. By making this arrangement, you have put yourself in a phase just like the phases of the moon. You are allowing yourself to change and to grow.

3. Touch each crystal one by one and say:

   I activate my will.
   I will myself to (speak your intention out loud).
   As I will, so must it be.
   And I will (this is an affirmative statement, a promise to yourself).

4. Write down the affirmations in your book.
5. Repeat as the candle burns down and allow the charm to grow into a chant. The resonating vibrations of your voice will align the crystals with your will. You may leave the crescent on your altar or gather the stones in a pouch and keep them with you whenever you need to remind yourself to act in accordance with your will.

CRYSTAL CONNECTION SPELL

It is easy to feel disconnected from yourself at times. Life pulls you in so many different directions that you can get lost in expectations and obligations and find yourself unexpectedly separated from your true nature as a witch. You might even feel compelled to conceal or contain your magickal side at times, depending on your surroundings and whether the people around you are open-minded or supportive or not. This simple spell will help restore your connection to your craft, your path, and renew your magickal energy.

Crystal Connection Spell

In this spell you will need to know which element corresponds to your sign. Use this table to find which element corresponds to your sun sign and own it.

Earth	Air	Fire	Water
Taurus Virgo Capricorn	Gemini Libra Aquarius	Aries Leo Sagittarius	Cancer Scorpio Pisces

You Will Need

- Quiet place for contemplation
- Any crystal from the hexagonal system that presents as a six-sided prism

Directions

1. Hold the crystal in your left hand and close your eyes. The left hand is your "receiving" hand. By holding the crystal in your left hand, you are opening yourself to engaging with its power.
2. With the first and middle fingers of your right hand, touch *one* of the crystal faces. As your fingers from your right hand come into contact with the crystal, give this facet a name that reflects one aspect of yourself in this moment. It could be your astrological sign or your elemental sign. Use your magickal name if you have one, or use your given name. As you move your fingers across the crystal plane, say:

   I am (NAME) of the (ZODIAC) sun.

3. Turn the crystal over in your hand to reveal a new facet that faces up.
4. Touch the crystal with the same two fingers and connect with your elemental sign:

   I am of the (choose one: earth, air, fire, water).

5. Turn the crystal over to touch a new facet. Speak the place from where your power originates. Choose as many as are true for you:

   My power rises through
   The liminal
   The horned ones
   The hoofed ones
   The night creatures
   The plants
   The herbs
   The kitchen
   The hedge
   The ocean
   The rivers
   The deep earth
   The stones
   The stars
   The celestial
   The mothers
   The daughters
   Time itself

6. Repeat this exploration of connection by reciting from the previous list until you have touched all six of the crystal faces and spoken your connections to magick out loud as you touch each face of the crystal. Keep the crystal with you and touch it whenever you start to feel disconnected or simply when you are called to step into your power.

CRYSTAL WISDOM MATRIX SPELL

As a witch, you may feel pulled in many different directions at once. Balancing a magickal path with the necessities and obligations of daily life can be a real challenge. Constructing and, more importantly, interacting with this matrix will help illuminate your priorities, ground you, and bring you back to center, all while making your next steps crystal clear.

Crystal Wisdom Matrix Spell

You Will Need

- Six-sided crystal tower prism, any type that resonates with you
- 6 smaller crystals, either rough or tumbled stones. Suggestions are:
  - Your birthstone, representing your relationship to yourself
  - Smoky quartz, representing your home or your environment where you feel grounded
  - Iolite, representing your responsibilities and obligations
  - Lapis lazuli, representing family and/or past life connections
  - Aventurine, representing your creative energy
  - Selenite, representing your spirituality or psychic abilities

Directions

1. Place the tower on your altar. Surround the tower with the six crystals so that each crystal is touching a different face of the tower.
2. Touch the tip of the tower with the first finger of your right hand while simultaneously touching your third eye with the first finger of your left hand. Invoke alignment by speaking out loud:

   As it is above, so be it below.

3. Next, touch each individual crystal and call it by name. This name is the aspect of yourself and your life that the crystal is representing:

   My birthstone, myself
   Smoky quartz, my grounded and protected home
   Iolite, my responsibilities and obligations
   Lapis lazuli, my family and those behind me
   Aventurine, my creative energy and that which is before me
   Selenite, my mind's eye.

4. Now you have connected your life to the above and below through contact with the tower. Observe where the crystals touch the tower and begin to slide each crystal away from the tower by how much time you devote to any of those endeavors. The crystals that are farthest away are the aspects that you engage with most frequently.
5. Look at the matrix and meditate on the following questions: Which places are you in control of? Which aspects have you been neglecting? What is in need of your attention? Where is your energy going?
6. Observe and make any adjustments. Go forward with new self-knowledge and wisdom and with the power to move your life in the direction you need it to go. Think about the crystals that are still the closest to the tower and think about ways to engage more fully with your life. Leave the matrix on your altar and adjust the placement of the stones as you change and adjust your priorities. Be passionate about yourself even as you are shifting and changing.

CRYSTAL CHAKRA IMBALANCE REVEALER SPELL

Before you can balance your chakras, keeping your etheric body in alignment with your corporeal form, you need to be able to determine where any imbalances may be lurking. You may have an adept clairvoyant read your chakras, or you can use crystals to tune in to your own intuition and do it yourself. Identifying blocks is the first step to addressing and correcting them.

Crystal Chakra Imbalance Revealer Spell

Note: In this spell, it is important that these crystals are as clear as possible. Each of these crystal types exhibits transparency, and it is essential that they are able to refract light.

You Will Need

- White candle
- Crystal pyramid, tower, or sphere

- 7 tumbled or rough crystals:
  - Red garnet
  - Citrine
  - Heliodor (golden beryl or golden feldspar)
  - Prasiolite
  - Aquamarine
  - Iolite
  - Amethyst

Directions

1. Light the candle and place the pyramid (or tower or sphere) in front of the candle.
2. Hold the garnet in front of the flame and observe your feelings. Pay attention to your intuition, then put the garnet down beside the pyramid.
3. Take the citrine, then the heliodor, and repeat gazing through the crystal as you hold it in front of the candle; place the crystals on your altar one at a time.
4. You should be looking at a row of three crystals in front of the pyramid.
5. Next, repeat the process with the prasiolite, aquamarine, and iolite. Hold each one in front of the candle and gaze at the light through it. Then make another row above the garnet, citrine, and heliodor.
6. Finally, take the amethyst and hold it in front of the candle. Gaze through it and acknowledge your intuition. Pay particular attention to how you feel and what you see. Place the amethyst alone and centered in front of the two rows of crystals.
7. Now close your eyes and touch the sides of the pyramid with as many of your fingers from both hands as you can. Breathe into your center and picture the ascending pyramid in your mind as you touch it.
8. Next, with your eyes remaining closed, hold your hands over the ordered crystals, hovering just above them. See if you can feel subtle variations in their energy.
9. Lay your hands on top of the crystals with your eyes remaining closed. Now you are ready to start moving them.
10. Without opening your eyes, but relying wholly on your clairvoyance or psychic sight, move the crystals into a single vertical line. Once you have moved a crystal, do not touch it again. When you have ordered all the crystals, take a look at the line and notice the placements.

11. Is the amethyst closest to the pyramid? Then your crown chakra is in alignment.
12. Each crystal is connected to a chakra through sympathetic magick. The colors of the crystals align with the colors associated with each chakra. By moving the crystals according to your intuition, you are revealing needs and strengths as they are presently affecting you. Are your lower chakras in order, or are they crowded and uneven? The way you have intuitively placed them will reveal the way you feel about your survival, sex, and your will. Are they bumping up against each other, out of order? Or do they have room to expand? See if you can make any correlations in your life. Is your housing situation secure? Are you able to give and receive pleasure? Do you know what you want and do you have some idea of how to get it? If you feel a pull in your intuition that says "yes," then you are probably in alignment. If your intuition tells you "no," then this indicates a block.
13. Once you have read your lower chakras, start interpreting the next three. Is your heart in the right place, or is it caught in your throat? Is your third eye out of order? Examine how you have interacted with your crystals to see where you need to be focusing your attention right now. The crystals are the tactile link between your intuition, your etheric body, and your corporeal body. After you have a new understanding of your etheric body through crystal wisdom, you are ready to take the next steps to bring yourself back to a more balanced state.

LAYING OF STONES CRYSTAL SPELL

Placing crystals directly onto your body is a powerful way to attune your energy. Direct contact of crystals to skin can stimulate healing. Some witches may use warm stones to create a relaxing effect. You may use the same crystals that you used for revealing your chakra imbalances and give them contact with your body. This encourages you to lie still, meditate, engage with your intuition, and relax to bring about peace and well-being. You can do this alone or with a partner, depending on how comfortable you are sharing your body and whether you are partnered or not. For the Laying of Stones, you may lie on your stomach and have your partner place the stones on you, or you may lie on your back and do it yourself.

Laying of Stones Crystal Spell

You Will Need

- Comfortable place to lie flat
- 7 crystals, one of each color: red, orange, yellow, green, blue, indigo, and violet

Directions

1. With your legs closed and your back straight, place the red crystal at the base of your spine if you are on your back (your partner can do this for you), or if you are supine, place it at the top of where your thighs come together.
2. Meditate on your abilities. Engage with your survival instincts. Congratulate yourself on making it this far.
3. Take the orange crystal and place it 4–6 inches above the red crystal. Breathe deeply and engage with your fertility, your power to attract, your life force, and feelings of desire and pleasure. If you are called to a state of arousal, go with it and view it as a sacred expression of your life force and your power to create.
4. Take the yellow crystal and place it on your body 4 inches above your navel, or if you are working with a partner and you are lying on your stomach, have your partner place it on the middle of your back. Breathe into your power, the things that you are able to manifest and make happen in the world. Here is where you engage with the things that you want and that you have the power to make happen.
5. Take the green crystal and place it centered on your chest, or have your partner place it between your shoulder blades if you are lying facedown. Breathe into your heart level with love. Allow yourself to be awash in love as it rains down around and within you, permeating your being with the crystal functioning as the touch point through which you may allow yourself to feel deep and lasting love.
6. Take the blue crystal and place it either at your throat or have your partner place it on the back of your neck. As you breathe, allow yourself to vocalize. This doesn't have to be verbal. You can hum, exhale with a vowel sound, or use a mantra if that is part of your practice. The important thing is to use your voice. Breathe into the sound of your power and allow channels of communication to open. These can be interpersonal, divine, or spiritual channels, or links within yourself.

7. Take the indigo crystal and place it between your eyes or have your partner balance it on the back of your head. This is the realm of your psychic sight, and you will breathe into your spiritual gifts. Center yourself in your intuition and accept yourself as a clairvoyant, psychic, powerful witch.
8. Penultimately, take the purple crystal and place it so that it is touching the top of your head. Breathe into the feeling of ascension into the higher places. You may feel a sense of extreme peace or even exhilaration. Meditate on your connections to spirits, the energy that inhabits the rocks and trees, oceans, streams, and rivers, and extend your knowledge of this life force so that it expands beyond your physical body. Allow your eternal soul and spirit to touch the divine energy surrounding you.
9. Finally, allow yourself to feel all seven of the open and flowing energy centers at once. You might feel pulled by a few of them. Continue to breathe and feel where the crystals touch your body. Imagine a swirling vortex of power at each touch point that can dilate and open to receive blessings and wisdom. When you have received the full benefit of the balancing, remove the stones from your body and be gentle with yourself. Do some deep breathing and touch the ground or floor to remain centered and calm.

Chapter 10

CRYSTALS by the CALENDAR

Crystals are the receptacles of time itself. And over time, human beings have ascribed greater and greater significance to certain crystals that have specific connections to certain times of the year. There is much to be gained by learning which crystals are most auspicious at certain times of the day, week, month, and year. Exploring these connections and correlations will deepen your understanding of natural history as well as human history.

THE CONNECTION BETWEEN CRYSTALS AND TIME

Humans have a natural tendency to imbue the world with meaning, and crystals provide a gateway to understanding both the physical world and the metaphysical world as it manifests to us through the concept of time. Our understanding and experience of time is very different from the experience of crystal formation, which can develop over millions of years. Our lifespans are comparatively minute, but this does not make them any less wondrous. Crystals are our window to a world we will never experience: the deep past and the far future. And in the meantime, crystals are the way we are able to touch these places in the here and now that we may never otherwise explore.

The connection between crystals and time is prehistoric, but human beings have made the ancient into the immediate by allowing crystals to embody and represent specific increments of time. As early as the first century, special gems were used during a specific month. Today, modern equivalents of birthstones mirror this ancient practice. Crystals also have correlations to certain days. Just as our weekly calendar is associated with ancient gods and goddesses, these deities also have counterparts in our solar system to which we also connect crystal attributes. Furthermore, it is possible to develop crystal meditations for certain times of the day, tapping into the power of crystals to invigorate in the morning and provide a sense of calm in the evening. And the witch's calendar, also known as the Great Wheel or the Wheel of the Year, provides many meaningful opportunities to incorporate crystals into your practice of witchcraft.

EARLY CRYSTAL CORRELATIONS

During the first century, around C.E. 70, there is evidence that crystals and gems were used as a source of power. Although scholars are not in agreement as to the exact nature of these connections, it has been hypothesized that the idea of certain gems resonating with correlating months comes from the writing of a Jewish historian by the name of Flavius Josephus, who was the first to describe the Breastplate of Aaron. This legendary artifact is said to have contained twelve gems, one for each of the tribes of Israel. While any precise translation has been lost in the web of time and linguistic evolution, what is generally accepted and known is that the breastplate was worn over the heart by the high priest and that it provided protection as well as a means of communication with God. Depicted as a colorful grid of crystals hung about the neck, the Breastplate of Aaron provides some early insight as to how crystals were used in magick as a pathway to communicate with deity and for protective purposes too.

While scholars cannot say with certainty why these crystals and gems resonated so highly with these specific tribes or whether the names of these crystals and gems were correctly translated from the Torah, the crystal contents of the breastplate are generally accepted to be as follows in this list of the twelve tribes along with their associated crystals:

Levi Emerald	**Judah** Ruby	**Zebulun** Onyx
Simeon Peridot	**Asher** Topaz	**Issacher** Lapis lazuli
Reuben Carnelian	**Napthali** Amethyst	**Dan** Sapphire or zircon
Benjamin Green jasper or jade	**Joseph** Beryl	**Gad** Banded agate

The correlation between gems and the number twelve is believed to be the progenitor of the concept of birthstones, a tradition that has evolved over the centuries but is still widely affirmed today. Similar to a horoscope, which allows that certain attributes are granted to a person by nature of which constellations the sun was in during the time of their birth, the idea of a birthstone is that a person will have a particular affinity for a certain crystal depending on the month when they were born. Birthstones have been used as an expression of personal identity and have been given as tokens of recognition and love, and they are generally accepted to have a sentimental and positive impact on those who ascribe to them. Cultures across the world acknowledge the individual solar return with celebration, song, sweets, and simple spells. Blowing out a birthday candle and making a wish is incredibly similar to setting an intention and casting a manifestation spell. Using birthstones as a way to determine which crystals you may have a natural connection to is just as meaningful.

Birthstone Crystals of Ancient Rome

January Garnet	**February** Amethyst	**March** Bloodstone
April Sapphire	**May** Agate	**June** Emerald
July Onyx	**August** Carnelian	**September** Sardonyx
October Aquamarine	**November** Topaz	**December** Ruby

Zodiac Crystals of Ancient India

Kumbha Amethyst	**Meena** Aquamarine	**Mesha** Diamond
Vrushabha Emerald	**Mithuna** Pearl	**Karat or Kark** Ruby
Simha or Sinh Peridot	**Kanya** Sapphire	**Tula** Opal
Vrushchika Topaz	**Dhanu** Turquoise	**Makar** Garnet

Birthstone Crystals in the Modern United States

January Garnet	**February** Amethyst	**March** Aquamarine
April Diamond	**May** Emerald	**June** Alexandrite
July Ruby	**August** Peridot	**September** Sapphire
October Opal	**November** Topaz	**December** Turquoise

Zodiac Crystals of Western Astrology

Aquarius Garnet	**Pisces** Amethyst	**Aries** Bloodstone
Taurus Sapphire	**Gemini** Agate	**Cancer** Emerald
Leo Onyx	**Virgo** Carnelian	**Libra** Peridot
Scorpio Beryl	**Sagittarius** Topaz	**Capricorn** Ruby

Birthstones are based on the Julian calendar as well as the zodiac. The preceding tables of correspondence with their origins provide information on which crystals and gems (which are also crystals but distinguished as gems due to their relative rarity compared to other types of minerals) are auspicious for certain months. The ancient Roman and Hindu cultures are understood to have been the first to develop and name these connections. Western astrology adapted zodiac correspondences from these, and finally, the modern list of birthstones, which is still changing, was established in the early 1900s by adapting popular European associations and creating a somewhat standardized list.

THE MAGICK OF BIRTHSTONES

In the preceding tables, you may notice several overlaps in certain crystals, which are identical or adjacent to their earliest calendar associations. This is time's way of giving the modern witch permission to adapt these correlations according to their own intuition and intellect. Furthermore, collaboration among countries, cultures, and industries has expanded these correlations even further, offering alternative, more accessible crystals and gems. A cynical view of alternates and substitutes would center on the belief that lists are published to manipulate collectors into buying more. A sympathetic view would include the magickal tenet of "like attracting like" and the idea that crystals and gems with similar colors and composition may also have metaphysical properties in common. Remember that when working with crystals, knowledge adds to the depth of your spells because information can enrich your intention. Still, it is your intention that is most important, and this is something that really comes from deep within yourself. It can be very difficult to put complex emotions, situations, and desires into a short and snappy charm.

By gaining a wider understanding of similar energy, overlapping energy, and adjacent energy among crystal correlations, you will be able to use them more effectively. For example, say that you were born under the sign of Libra. Libra and the month of October correlate with opal; however, rose zircon and tourmaline (usually pink) are often used as substitutes. If you were interested in using crystal magick to invoke a year of prosperity, a green tourmaline variety would be the best crystal to use. Why? First of all, because opals are the most fragile of the three. Due to their delicate nature, which includes being inherently soft and subject to breakage, along with their water inclusions that make handling them with care necessary, there is a superstition attached to opals that a gift of an opal is bad luck. A fragile, although beautiful and rare, crystal is not going to be the best foundational crystal in a magickal working for manifesting prosperity. Opal, however, would be the appropriate choice for a person born under the sign of Libra or in the month of October if they were doing a spell on healing an emotional imbalance or seeking to engage with or fortify their vulnerable side.

There are other practical reasons for using alternates. Take the month of December, for example. Turquoise and topaz have both been associated with December. Turquoise is more commonly seen than topaz, and in the late 1900s, tanzanite was introduced as yet another alternate gem for the month of December. Now you have three crystal correlations, all of which are considered semiprecious, but topaz and tanzanite are far more expensive than a turquoise of comparable size. It might make sense for both your path and your budget to work with the more accessible crystals. Turquoise can be acquired for tens of dollars, while topaz and tanzanite can easily hit hundreds and thousands. Alternates are important.

Adjacent crystals are also important to know about. The Julian calendar and the zodiac can inform your choices about which crystals will resonate most strongly with your identity. Take the sign of Aquarius, for example. In Western astrology, the sun is in the constellation Aquarius January 20–February 19. An Aquarian born at the end of January might resonate more harmonically with amethyst than garnet. They might find the color more pleasing or the attributes of amethyst more in alignment with their craft goals or personal identity. Similarly, an Aquarian born at the end of February might be drawn to aquamarine more than amethyst. If a certain crystal correlation doesn't seem to "fit" your idea of yourself, explore the charts and tables to find alternates and adjacents.

Zodiac Crystals: Additionals, Alternates, and Adjacents

Aquarius January 20–February 19 Turquoise, amethyst, onyx, labradorite, jade, aquamarine	**Pisces** February 20–March 20 Aquamarine, amethyst, moonstone, rose quartz, sugilite	**Aries** March 21–April 20 Carnelian, ruby, jasper, aquamarine, hematite
Taurus April 21–May 21 Topaz, tiger's eye, rose quartz, tourmaline	**Gemini** May 22–June 22 Citrine, agate, calcite, apophyllite, tourmaline	**Cancer** June 23–July 23 Carnelian, moonstone, amber, chrysoprase, pearl
Leo July 24–Aug 23 Peridot, sardonyx, ruby, sunstone, fire agate, amber	**Virgo** August 24–September 23 Lapis lazuli, peridot, rutilated quartz, carnelian, moonstone	**Libra** September 24–October 23 Rose quartz, apophyllite, aquamarine, jade, peridot, aventurine, tourmaline
Scorpio October 24–November 22 Citrine, topaz, malachite, obsidian, opal, turquoise	**Sagittarius** November 23–December 20 Blue lace agate, labradorite, malachite, topaz, turquoise, garnet	**Capricorn** December 21–January 19 Garnet, onyx, jet, smoky quartz, clear quartz, green tourmaline, black tourmaline

ZODIAC IDENTITY SPELL

Now that you have a sense of which crystals you may have an affinity for based on the time of year that you arrived on the planet, you can use this information to build a personal charm that can aid you in your process of self-discovery. Your identity as a witch is a distillation of many different aspects of your personality and circumstances. You might be many things to different people: a sibling, a parent, a collaborator, a coven member, or a leader. Think about all the different aspects of yourself as you begin the following spell.

Zodiac Identity Spell

You Will Need

- A sacred space such as an altar or meditation mat where you can work undisturbed
- White candle
- Clear quartz crystal
- Stick of incense
- Incense holder
- 3 crystals: 1 representing your birth month, 1 representing your zodiac sign, and 1 that you have an affinity for, which is determined by your own personal preferences
- Small velvet or muslin pouch big enough to hold all 3 crystals
- Slip of paper
- Pen or pencil

Directions

1. Light the candle and place the clear quartz in front of it. Silently or speaking aloud, reflect on the following affirmation:

   I am passionate about myself, even while I am changing. I name this crystal "Clarity" in honor of myself in this moment.

2. Light the stick of incense. This will be your measure of time. A 6-inch stick will generally burn for about thirty minutes. You will spend the next thirty minutes holding and reflecting on the energy of each crystal, spending about ten minutes focusing on each one.
3. Start with your birthstone crystal. Hold it in your hands and repeat the following affirmation, adapting it to personalize it to your experience:

   I hold the month of ____________ in my hand, and all the promise that it brings. At my solar return, I am born anew.

4. Watch the incense stick. As it burns down, think about the season when you were born and all of the things that you value about that time of year. Each distinct season has its particular joys, and these are the energy signature of your arrival.
5. Name them aloud. Decide which ones you will keep close to your heart and use them in a series of "I am" statements. These are all just examples of how one aspect of the month when you were born can inform your identity as a witch. For example:

I am January of the Deep Cold.
I am February of the Quickening.
I am March of the Miracle of Spring.
I am April of the Gentle Rains that Nourish and Cleanse.
I am May of the Hawthorn Blossoms.
I am June of the Leafing Oak.
I am July of the Summer Sun.
I am August of the First Harvest.
I am September of the Golden Wheat.
I am October of the Falling Leaves.
I am November of the Coming Cold.
I am December of the Longest Nights.

6. After you have made your "I am" statement, you can add on a "my" statement. For example:

    January: *My winds of change bring unexpected treasures.*
    February: *My turning point brings in new energy.*
    March: *My strength is the balance point.*
    April: *My peace is my power.*
    May: *My passion is my power.*
    June: *My triumph is the sun.*
    July: *My dreams are valid.*
    August: *My hopes are strong.*
    September: *My harvest is bountiful.*
    October: *My endings are beginnings.*
    November: *My golden light persists.*
    December: *My peace is felt by all.*

7. Repeat your "I am" statement and link it to your "my" statement as you reflect on your identity and your attributes.

8. When ten minutes are up (you will know this because the incense stick will have burned about ⅓ of the way down), pick up the pouch and give it a little swish above the incense. Put you birth month crystal inside the pouch.

9. Reach for your zodiac crystal and repeat the process with "I am" and "my." For example:

I am the Water Bearer. My inspiration pours over the land.
I am the Fish. My power lies in my ability to flow.
I am the Ram. My energy is formidable and strong.
I am the Bull. My sacred nature is revered throughout the ages.
I am the Twins. My nature is mutable and flexible.
I am the Crab. My safety is my shell.
I am the Lion. My voice is respected.
I am the Virgin. My strength is clarity.
I am the Scales. My quest for balance endures.
I am the Scorpion. My sting protects me.
I am the Centaur. My aim is true.
I am the Sea Goat. My shape-shifting magick allows me to enter any world.

10. Take your ten minutes to repeat your affirmations together and put your zodiac crystal in the pouch together with your birth month crystal. Then take the final crystal, the one you chose for yourself for your own personal reasons, and reflect on it as the incense stick burns down. Notice its color. Notice its texture. Notice its temperature as it attunes itself to your touch. Notice its weight. Turn it over. As you do this, think about the aspect of your identity that is the most important to you and call yourself by this identity and then compliment yourself. For example:

    I am an adept scholar. Knowledge is mine.
    I am a trusted friend. Secrets are safe with me.
    I am a beloved mother. Love is my law.
    I am a creative artist. Inspiration is my power.
    I am a fantastic lover. All who know my touch are blessed.

11. Finally, you will end with the phrase, "I am a sacred witch. I claim my power." Put the last crystal in the pouch with the other two.
12. Use the pen or pencil to write the charm on the paper. You should have three "I am" statements followed by two "my" statements and a final personal aspect statement phrased as a compliment.
13. Place the paper in front of the candle and pass the clear crystal over the words. You should see the words "dance" through the crystal.
14. Hold the paper in front of the candle (not too close, you are not going to ignite the paper) so that the candle illuminates the paper. Fold the

paper and place it in the pouch with the three crystals. Blow out the candle.

15. You can keep these three crystals in your pocket, you can sleep with them under your pillow, you can hold them and take them out and touch them anytime you need a confidence boost or whenever you are feeling unsure and just need to remember the powerful, emerging, changing, growing, sacred witch that you are.

The Day, the Month, and the Hour

Consider making yourself a crystal charm bag that contains a crystal each to represent the hour, the day, the month, and the time of year when you were born. If you have a friend who is also interested in crystals, consider gifting them with their own personal crystal charm bag and explain why you chose each one. This could be a meaningful gift that could inspire the personal power of someone special to you.

CRYSTALS AROUND THE CLOCK

Incorporating crystals into your daily waking and evening routines is a powerful way to set your intentions, increase your vitality, and finally ground and center yourself at the end of the day. Your observances need not be particularly complex, but with consistency you may find that adding crystals to your waking and retiring routines infuses your day with extra magick. This is the nature of how ritual impacts magick: Simple acts performed repeatedly gain power and change the practitioner for the better if they are done correctly and with care. Think of something as simple as brushing your teeth. If you do it multiple times every day, you will most likely remain in good dental health. If you brush only sometimes, you will always gain the benefit of what you do, but not the full benefit of what you could be experiencing. Morning and evening meditation with crystals are no different. They become part of your day, a beautiful part that gives a touch of magick to the mundane. And incorporating a daily crystal routine is even easier than brushing your teeth. Here is a simple way to use crystals as the "bookends" for your day.

Crystals Around the Clock Spell

For this spell you will be using two crystal pairs of contrasting small crystal spheres or tumbled stones, no smaller than 1 inch but no larger than 1½ inches in diameter. The important thing is that they are smooth, there are no points or rough edges, and they can fit in the palm of your hand. Some choices might be:

- A pair of yellow or light-colored crystal spheres or tumbled stones. Choose either two agates, two rose quartz spheres, or two citrine spheres. The crystals should match each other, but it is not imperative that they do so. For example, if you want to start your day with love and light, choose one rose quartz and one citrine.
- A pair of dark or opaque crystal spheres or tumbled stones. Choose either onyx, dark amethyst, jasper, or obsidian.

Again, you will gain a certain amount of focus from the visual symmetry of a matched pair, but say your intention is to ground your energy and engage with your subconscious through dreams, which would then make jasper and a dark opaque amethyst an appropriate pair.

You Will Need

- Small box capable of holding 2 pairs of crystals
- 2 pairs of crystals (see previous direction)
- Small white cloth that can cover the light pair of crystals
- Small black cloth that can cover the dark pair of crystals

Directions

1. Keep the box near your bedside. You do not need any special invocations or magick words.
2. In the morning when you wake up, unwrap the two light crystals and imagine how you wish the events of your day to unfold. Hold one crystal in each hand and think about what you would like to come to you, what you will accept, and what you would prefer. Keep your eyes closed and just concentrate on the crystals in your hand.

3. Think on these three attributes as you close your eyes and breathe deeply:

   "I invoke (your intention for the day)." *It can be a single word, an affirming phrase, or a specific wish. For example: "I invoke peace." Or "I invoke success."*

   "I need (your highest hope for just this day)." *It can be a pleasant interaction, or a focus on what you want to occur. For example: "I need acknowledgement." Or "I need to be punctual." This is your time to determine your immediate emotional needs for the day.*

   "I accept (what you are willing to invite into your reality)." *For example: "I accept compliments." Or "I accept grace." This is where you make room for positive experiences to come to you today.*

4. Then wrap the crystals in the white cloth and put them back into the box and go about your daily activities.
5. In the evening or when it is time for you to wind down, before you retire to sleep, take the dark crystals out of the box. Unwrap them and hold one in each hand. Think about the events of the day and allow yourself some time to process and decompress. Think about the things that went right and the things that did not. Allow your mind to release any stress or lingering negativity by letting your crystals do their work. Close your eyes and take several deep breaths as you focus on these three affirmations:

   "I gained (these are the interactions or experiences that you had that were in alignment with your intention and hope *no matter how small*)!" *Here, you are using the crystals as grounding tools with which to accept what came through the opening you created in the morning. For example: "I gained nourishment" if you were fortunate enough to enjoy a preferred meal. Or "I gained understanding" if you were able to make your voice heard at any point in the day.*

   "I release (these are the things you are letting go of *right now at this moment*)." *If you are holding on to lingering upset due to unpleasant interactions that happened earlier, let them go right now. Do not carry them forward into your dream time. For example, "I release my frustration."*

   "I return (this is where you name your "reset" activity as you feel the crystals gaining warmth in your hand)." *For example, "I return to the source." Or "I return to my dreams." Or "I return to rest."*

6. Remember, these affirmations do not need to be spoken aloud. Since you are holding your crystals while engaging in this small ritual, you are experiencing an earth connection, an emotional connection, and a magickal connection. These connections will strengthen with time. Place your dark crystals back in their cloth and allow yourself to enter into a restful dream state. Repeat as often as you feel necessary.

AUSPICIOUS CRYSTALS FOR EACH DAY OF THE WEEK

Now that you have a morning and evening crystal routine, here is another way you can incorporate crystal magick day by day. Many people understand that the way we experience time is connected to ancient beliefs in magick and deity. Planets of our solar system were named after Roman gods, while we count the seven days of the week by naming a mix of Roman planetary and Nordic deities. It might not always be top of mind, but each calendar week has some correlation with celestial and mythological significance. The sun; the moon; the gods Tyr, Odin, Thor; the goddess Freya; and the god/planet Saturn mark each day as you move through the week. Each of these entities—planetary, celestial, and immortal—has corresponding crystals. You can use these correspondences to your advantage when taking any action with intention. Life will bring many high-stakes moments where decisions have to be made, crises must be navigated, and confrontations have to be resolved. Knowing how to magickally plan your week and which crystals will be most effective on certain days can strengthen your resolve and hone your focus.

If you are bound to the workweek, like many people are, you may notice that certain days pick up negative energy signatures because so many people are repeating these ideas, giving them power. Instead of Monday being filled with drudgery and dread, use crystals to associate Monday with the moon! Instead of Wednesday taking on the energy of a slump day or "hump day," use a crystal to remind you of the strength and power of Odin, the All-Father. And while everyone else is celebrating with trite sayings like "Thank God it's Friday," you can use a crystal to remind you to thank the goddess Freya as well so that you can remain in tune and in touch with magickal energy every day of the week.

Crystals by the Day

Sunday: Sun	**Monday:** Moon	**Tuesday:** Tyr	**Wednesday:** Odin
Sunstone Citrine Heliodor	Moonstone Selenite	Smoky quartz Hematite	Agate Carnelian Jet Onyx
Thursday: Thor	**Friday:** Freya	**Saturday:** Saturn	
Lodestone Carnelian Clear quartz Aquamarine	Rose quartz Amber Pyrite Jade Malachite	Sapphire Lapis lazuli Iolite	

CRYSTALS TO ATTUNE WITH SABBATS AND SEASONS

Many witches celebrate the Wheel of the Year as a way to attune with the changing seasons. The Wheel of the Year is observed by Wiccans and other religious witches who may or may not identify as Wiccan. There are also many seasonal traditions that are central to Wheel of the Year observances that are secular traditions as well. A perfect example is Imbolc. Witches celebrate Imbolc in February as a time of initiation. Candles are lit and neophytes progress from the outer court to the inner court of the coven. Solitary witches may observe Imbolc by creating a Brigid's Cross from reeds and light candles. There might be prayers and offerings to Cailleach (the divine hag goddess who rules over winter) and prognostications as to whether or not spring will arrive early. In the secular world, Groundhog Day is observed with generally the same intent: to predict weather outcomes in the near future. A secular witch might light candles to represent the return of the light and acknowledge that the planet is now at a point in time that is halfway between winter and spring. Using crystals that correlate with the themes of initiation, rebirth, and light returning can sanctify an altar or raise the energy of an environment.

Samhain is another perfect example, revered around the world as Halloween, Day of the Dead, and All Souls' Day. People of diverse cultural backgrounds and diverse faiths are all celebrating similar themes at the same time of year. And the secular world is no exception. You will find no greater interest in witchcraft than around Halloween, which is also the Witch's New Year. Themes of endings, spirits, haunting, and a thinning of the veil between the living and the dead are the prevalent themes. It stands to reason that crystals such as onyx and obsidian with their dark and reflective surfaces, together with adularescent stones such as moonstone and selenite, would be auspicious at the end of October and dawn of November.

Many people think the Wheel of the Year is ancient. It is not. The celebration of the Wheel of the Year is very modern. Yes, some of these holidays are ancient, but not all of them. The four Celtic fire festivals are perhaps the best known, as are the solstices and equinoxes, but not all equinoxes were celebrated in ancient times, and Mabon, an observance for witches, was added in the late twentieth century to balance out the Wheel. It is entirely in line with modern witchcraft to adapt, adopt, and balance rituals. Combining crystals with a secular or sacred practice is legitimate even though it isn't ancient. The wonderful thing about crystals and correspondences is that they are powerful whether you believe in them or not! A secular witch will get a benefit just as will a religious witch from having auspicious crystals accessible at certain points of the year. Use the following tables to choose crystals for your altar, for your person, or for your pocket, or to display and attune with the energy of the season. Feel your strength, beauty, and power rise!

Crystals for Sabbats

Samhain	**Yule**	**Imbolc**	**Ostara**
Jet	Malachite	Quartz	Fluorite
Onyx	Carnelian	Selenite	Tourmaline
Obsidian	Garnet	Moonstone	Azurite
Bloodstone	Snowflake obsidian	White agate	Aquamarine
Moonstone	Jade		Rhodolite
Selenite			
Beltane	**Litha**	**Lughnasad**	**Mabon**
Rhodochrosite	Fluorite	Amber	Peridot
Garnet	Sunstone	Carnelian	Topaz
Peridot	Heliodor	Jasper	Smoky quartz
Ametrine	Citrine	Tiger's Eye	Moss agate
Ruby	Aventurine		

Crystals for Seasons

Spring	Summer	Winter	Autumn
Fluorite	Aventurine	Quartz	Carnelian
Rose quartz	Amazonite	Selenite	Agate
Prasiolite	Heliodor	Azurite	Jasper
Tourmaline	Citrine	Aquamarine	Chalcedony
Apatite	Malachite	Moonstone	Amber

CRYSTALS BY CANDLELIGHT

When the sun sets and you find yourself in the twilight and the calm of approaching darkness surrounds you, you can use crystals to bring about an instant state of peace by pairing a few small-to-medium clusters with a simple votive candle. Like with an evening vesper, you can choose either to meditate in silence or to listen to a simple harmonic interval or soothing music.

Crystal Spell for Peace

You Will Need

- Votive candle
- Small glass candleholder or jar
- 5 medium crystals ranging from 1 inch × 2 inches to 3 inches × 4 inches

Directions

1. Clear an altar or a small shelf and surrounding surface area. Place the votive in the holder or jar and place it in the center, then light it.
2. Take the first crystal and lean it against the glass. Take the second crystal and lean it against the glass and the first crystal. It can take a little bit of time to find the balance points and how they work together.
3. While you explore the relationships between the lit candle and the two crystals, pay attention to the details. Notice where they touch. Decide if balance is only possible because they must lean on each other. Contemplate the nature of your relationships. What or who could these crystals represent?

4. Continue placing and balancing the remaining three crystals. Ask yourself who is in your community. Think about the interactions you had throughout the day. Take stock of who you are and what you have and allow yourself to experience gratitude.
5. Notice the ways that the crystals interact with light. Adjust them to maximize the light play. Place them so that the light can transmit to your eye through reflection and concentrate on areas of dispersed light as well.
6. Once you are satisfied with your placement, listen to your preferred music or sound and enjoy the magickal environment you have created and allow your candle to burn down.

MANIFESTATION SPELL OF THE THIRTEEN MOONS

Each lunar cycle has a special attribute. You can incorporate the power of the moon as its aspects change throughout the year in order to bring about your desires. Crystals can help aid your manifestation because they can correlate and amplify the power of the moon, which you will draw down into yourself in order to manifest. This spell is ideal for manifesting things that align with the calendar year, such as a handfasting, which lasts for a year and a day or for the year in which it takes a neophyte witch to become an acolyte.

Manifestation Spell of the Thirteen Moons

You Will Need

- 13 tea light candles
- Carnelian to represent the Blood Moon (October)
- Snowflake obsidian to represent the Snow Moon (November)
- Jet to represent the Dark Moon (December)
- Clear quartz to represent the Cold Moon (January)
- Selenite to represent the Wild Moon (February)
- Labradorite to represent the Storm Moon (March)
- Onyx to represent the Seed Moon (April)
- Rhodochrosite to represent the Hare Moon (May)
- Amber to represent the Mead Moon (June)

- Agate to represent the Wort Moon (July)
- Citrine to represent the Barley Moon (August)
- Topaz to represent the Harvest Moon (September)

Directions

1. Arrange the tea lights in a circle. As you place them, set your intention for the year.
2. Begin placing the crystals inside of the circle of candles one by one, starting with the carnelian. As you place each crystal, recite the charm:

   Stone of one, the spell has begun
   Stone of two, my aim is true
   Stone of three, so mote it be
   Stone of four, it's strengthened more
   Stone of five, the spell will thrive
   Stone of six, the spell I fix
   Stone of seven, blessed by heaven
   Stone of eight, the hand of fate
   Stone of nine, (YOUR INTENTION) is mine
   Stone of ten, will show me when
   Stone of eleven, reveal the succession
   Stone of twelve, in magick I delve
   Stone of thirteen, my outcome is seen.

3. Light the candles one by one so that all of your moon crystals are protected by a ring of fire. Imagine that anything that threatens to thwart your desire must first encounter the flames, where it is turned to ash. Meditate on the candlelight for as long as you wish. Carry each crystal with you or set it on your altar during the full moon of that month.

CRYSTALS BY THE HOUR SPELL

Crystals can empower your spells and rituals throughout the year, but they can also be used to make any hour of the day infused with magick. You can use these crystals to attune with the hour of birth or a handfasting or wedding. They are even useful for mundane events.

Suppose you have a meeting or an interview or some other high-stakes encounter that is set for a particular time of day. You can use crystals to focus and concentrate your power, which can improve the chances of success.

Crystals by the Hour Spell

For this spell you will need to choose a crystal for the hour of your birth or the hour of importance. Here is a list to help you:

- Clear quartz to represent 1:00 a.m.
- Hematite to represent 2:00 a.m.
- Malachite to represent 3:00 a.m.
- Lapis lazuli to represent 4:00 a.m.
- Turquoise to represent 5:00 a.m.
- Tourmaline to represent 6:00 a.m.
- Chrysoprase to represent 7:00 a.m.
- Amethyst to represent 8:00 a.m.
- Kunzite to represent 9:00 a.m.
- Sapphire to represent 10:00 a.m.
- Garnet to represent 11:00 a.m.
- Citrine to represent noon
- Smoky quartz to represent 1:00 p.m.
- Emerald to represent 2:00 p.m.
- Beryl to represent 3:00 p.m.
- Topaz to represent 4:00 p.m.
- Ruby to represent 5:00 p.m.
- Opal to represent 6:00 p.m.
- Agate to represent 7:00 p.m.
- Chalcedony to represent 8:00 p.m.
- Jade to represent 9:00 p.m.
- Jasper to represent 10:00 p.m.
- Lodestone to represent 11:00 p.m.
- Onyx to represent midnight

You Will Need

- Crystal for the hour of your birth or the hour of importance (see previous instruction)
- Timekeeping device such as your phone or your wristwatch or a clock
- Small velvet pouch

Directions

1. Take the crystal that represents the auspicious hour and touch it to your timepiece. As you hold it there, close your eyes and envision your desired outcome. This could be anything, such as an uneventful dentist appointment; a successful job interview; an enjoyable date; a punctual arrival at a function, or school, or work, or any time-bound endeavor no matter how great or small.
2. While you keep the crystal in contact with your device, recite or meditate on the charm:

   By my word and by my deed
   At the fateful hour
   I will fulfill my greatest need
   And use the crystal's power.

3. Take the crystal off of your device and place it in the velvet pouch. Keep it with you as you move in the direction of your destiny and dreams.

CRYSTAL CALENDAR COMBINING SPELL

Whether you decide to use the Crystals by the Hour Spell for something of great importance or something for which you just need a little power in your corner, you can combine this crystal spell with crystals from the Crystals by the Day table to make your intention even more specific.

Crystal Calendar Combining Spell

For this spell you will choose a crystal from the list in the preceeding Crystals by the Hour Spell that matches the time of day that you need to feel empowered. You can also choose several crystals from the list so that you can plan to have the entire duration of the event covered.

For example, in order to give yourself a needed boost of aligned energy for an exam that you have to take on Wednesday from noon until 1:30 p.m., you would choose either agate, carnelian, jet, or onyx, depending on which crystal most closely aligns with your desired outcome, and combine it with citrine, quartz, and emerald to cover the entire time period.

You Will Need

- Incense
- White votive candle
- Cup of water
- Crystal that corresponds with the day on which you need to feel most empowered
- Crystal that closely matches the time when you need to feel empowered
- Charm bag or pouch large enough to accommodate 4–5 crystals

Directions

1. On your altar, place the incense, candle, water, and crystals.
2. Light the incense and pass the crystals through the smoke one by one.
3. Light the candle and hold each crystal around 6 inches above the flame, enough for you to feel some gentle heat but not enough to burn you. Make a small circular motion three times around the flame with each crystal.
4. Take each crystal and dip it in the water, then place it in the pouch, starting with the crystal representing the day, followed by the starting hour, and finally the ending hour.
5. Hold the pouch in your hands close to your heart and speak the charm:

   My will is my way
   On an auspicious day
   My will is my power
   At the fortunate hour.

6. Lick your fingers and pinch the candle out. Take the charm bag with you on the day that you need it and keep it as close as possible.

Chapter 11

CRYSTAL ARRANGEMENTS for ADVANCED MAGICK

Advanced altar craft can involve a variety of configurations. This chapter delves into meticulous intentional arrangements and the powerful manifestations that can result. Crystal matrix magick is rooted in the philosophy that there exists a plane of immanence that begins with a thought. This thought is born from the spark of creativity and determination. It is the intention of the witch that interacts with this place of becoming and begins the process of bringing the thought into manifestation in the physical realm. In this process the witch is the conduit and the crystals are her tools. In the infinite different configurations of the crystal matrix, you are able to get a glimpse of where the powers of heaven manifest on the earth. The geometry of repeating patterns is as sacred as any mantra, charm, or prayer. The act of arranging or creating a matrix puts a layer of physical touch in direct contact with powerful patterns. Intensely tactile and visual, creating matrices allows you to engage multiple senses and perhaps activate senses you didn't know you had.

SACRED GEOMETRY AND THE POWER OF PATTERNS

Earlier in the book, you engaged with many magickal systems used throughout the world, such as imitative magick, sympathetic magick, contagious magick, and contact magick. All of these aspects of practice are connected to sacred geometry. They all exist in a field on the plane of immanence. This is part of why crystal grids and matrices are so powerful: They are physical manifestations of the sacred ratios and patterns that govern the universe as we know it. Just as a rose blossom, pleasing to the eye and pleasing to the olfactory senses, will always have stations of five leaves along its stem, and a perfect fifth interval of music notes will be pleasing to the ear, so are the faces of a crystal pleasing to the touch as well as the eye. All of these things exist in our reality of manifestations of balance and pleasure. To tap into this unifying harmony, use the matrix of sacred geometry in the sublunar world.

Crystal Matrix of Sacred Geometry

You Will Need

- Working surface such as an altar or tabletop that can remain undisturbed for the period of the necessity (the time in between when you create the matrix and your intention begins to manifest)
- Crystal sphere or tower, chosen to represent your intention according to your need, or what you will bring into being in the here and now
- 8 clear quartz crystal points to connect immanence to intention
- 2 moonstone tumbled crystals to represent the lunar plane above you
- 2 labradorite tumbled crystals to represent the lunar plane above you
- 2 selenite tumbled crystals to represent the plane of heaven
- 2 celestite tumbled crystals to represent the plane of heaven

MATRIX *of* SACRED GEOMETRY

1. Tower or Sphere
2. Quartz
3. Labradorite
4. Moonstone
5. Selenite
6. Celestite

Directions

1. In the center of your altar, place the sphere or tower. Give it a name and speak the name aloud. The name is that which you are seeking. It can be a single word such as "healing" or "balance," or it can be as specific as "I need to manifest a new living situation in the next six weeks."
2. Next, place four of the clear points above, to the right, below, and to the left. Each of these will be given an action you will take. These actions should connect to what you seek. Speak these aloud as you place them. For example, if your goal is healing, you will name them after the things that you need to do in order for that healing to take place: engage in self-care, manage appointments, seek wisdom, investigate opinions.
3. Next, you will connect these actions to the higher plane by placing four additional crystals in the places in between. These you will also name according to your need and as a vow to act in accord. You might call them: "Meditate." " Lighten responsibilities." " Let go." " Lean in." Whatever it will take to activate your need and make it come to being is what you will speak aloud as you place these crystals.
4. Next, you will create the link to the lunar world. This is linking your intention to that celestial body, our only satellite. Use the moonstone and labradorite to frame the points like a compass rose indicating north, east, south, and west, representing the full and dark moons.

5. As you place these crystals, call upon the power of the tides, the pull of gravity that keeps the world in motion. Call upon these powers and let them connect to your actions, which will meet your intention.
6. Finally, you will delineate the square of heaven by blocking out the four points of the square, alternating with the selenite and the celestite. This is the realm of heaven above that you are linking to the lunar realm and then to the sublunar world, culminating in the manifestation of your intention.
7. Leave the matrix out for at least a lunar cycle or for as long as it takes you to make good on your promises to yourself and act in accord. Look for signs that your intention is manifesting and move accordingly.

ALTAR MATRIX FOR INVOKING

Spells and ritual will usually involve calling in energy of some kind no matter what the intended outcome may be. Whether you have the need to invoke deity, ancestors, elements, or spirits, creating an invoking matrix for your highest priority magickal workings will lend formality and importance to your requests. In creating an invoking matrix, you are essentially engaging with the surrounding field of energy to create an opening that good fortune, information, blessings, and success may flow through to you.

Altar Matrix for Invoking

In this spell, you can use a different mix of crystals to align with your purpose. This is a powerful matrix that will invoke love, clarity, and spiritual awakening. If your priority needs are different, feel free to change up the types of crystals but keep the number and shape the same. The flowers chosen here are to augment the crystals, providing a calm and loving backdrop for the invoking matrix. You may substitute other herbs or flowers or leave them out completely if they are not ideally suited to the magickal task at hand.

You Will Need

- 12 assorted small-to-medium tumbled or rough crystals, such as 2 rose quartz, 4 red garnet, 4 rhodolite garnet, and 2 rhodochrosite
- 14 small-to-medium crystal points, such as 7 clear quartz points and 7 amethyst points
- 6-inch plate
- 2 (18-inch) lengths of ribbon, yarn, or string
- ¼ cup dried lavender flowers
- ¾ cup dried rosebuds and/or rose petals

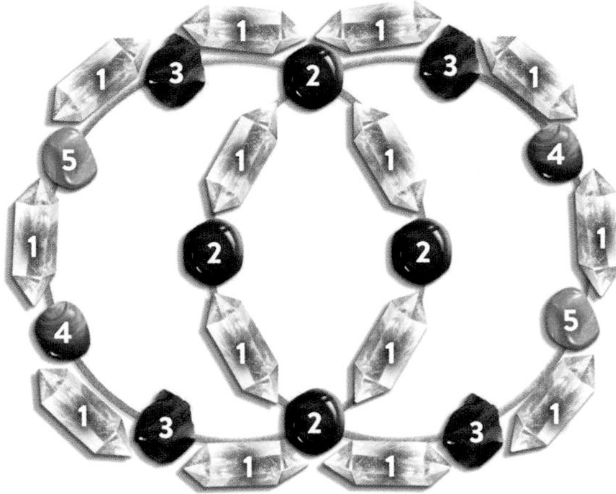

ALTAR MATRIX *for* INVOKING

1. Quartz
2. Red Garnet
3. Rhodolite
4. Rhodochrosite
5. Rose Quartz

Directions

1. Clear your altar and do a quick clean of the surface. Gather and clear your crystals. Charge them with your intention.
2. Take the plate and lay it facedown on your altar, offset to the left.
3. Take the ribbon or string and use it to encircle the circumference of the plate by laying it around the outer edge to give you a template for placing the crystals that you can easily remove without disturbing your placements.
4. Pick up the plate and move it to the right so that it is overlapping with the ribbon.
5. Use the second piece of ribbon to encircle the circumference of the plate by laying it around the outer edge.
6. Pick up the plate. You should be looking at a vesica piscis: two overlapping circles with an aperture in the place where they meet.

7. Take the four darkest red crystals and place them accordingly: two at the two places where the circles meet each other, two on the horizontal axis of the aperture.
8. Place the rest of the red crystals going from darkest to lightest around the outside perimeter of both circles.
9. Pick up the ribbons.
10. Use the crystal points to fill in the spaces in between the tumbled (or rough) crystals.
11. Add the lavender and rosebuds as an offering and a blessing to outline the vesica piscis.
12. Use the invoking matrix as a focal point in your meditations and as a manifesting activity to call to yourself the highest good that may be of benefit to all beings.
13. Leave the matrix on your altar for as long as it serves you.
14. When you take it down, pick up the crystals counter to the way you had placed them, picking up the outer circles first and the aperture last. Clear them and store them for future use. You can gather the herbs and use them as incense or just keep everything together in a muslin pouch and make a crystal bath or shower infusion.

The Power of Quartz

Quartz crystals (silicon dioxide) are among the most frequently occurring minerals on earth. Quartz will vibrate at specific frequencies when exposed to mechanical stress, such as compression, torsion, or bending. This internal resistance to outside forces makes them very important for electronics, hence the name "Silicon Valley" for one of the United States' primary locations for electronics development.

ALTAR MATRIX FOR PROTECTION

Protection is a real need. Many times you may find yourself feeling emotionally vulnerable or under attack. There are all manner of psychic attacks that a witch has to deal with. Cyberbullying, witch wars, flimsy accusations, gossip, and the like can all impinge on your peace of mind and inhibit your spiritual growth as well as your magick abilities. Casting a protective matrix puts you at the center of a shield and can serve as a powerful reminder that you are in control of how you react to things, that while righteous anger is justified, it doesn't have to rule you because you have the tools and skills to ward off psychic attacks and protect yourself. This matrix combines the protective power of the pentagram with the lambda, which was emblazoned on ancient Greek aspis shields. It is a powerful protective matrix that you can use as a ward during times of need.

Altar Matrix for Protection

Your altar is the physical representation of your witchcraft. It is the stage upon which you interact with the metaphysical realm. Use this matrix to protect it.

You Will Need

- Athame
- 3 jet or black obsidian crystals
- 3 tiger's eye crystals
- 5 carnelian crystals

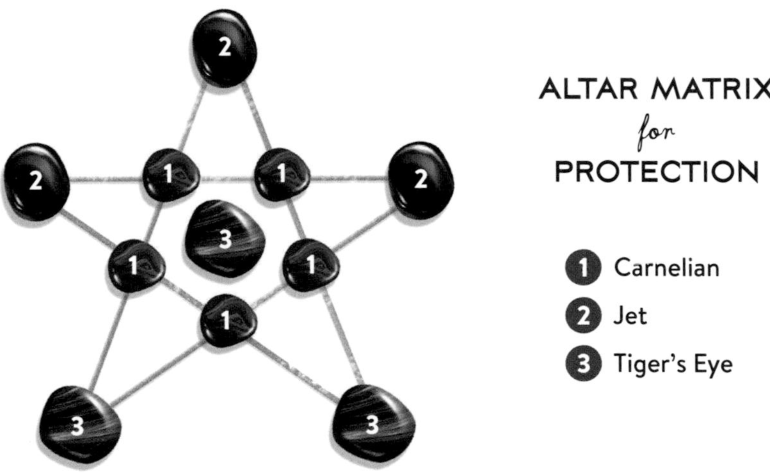

ALTAR MATRIX *for* PROTECTION

1. Carnelian
2. Jet
3. Tiger's Eye

Directions

1. On your altar, trace a pentagram with the tip of your athame.
2. Place the three black crystals at the top, right, and left points.
3. Place one tiger's eye in the center and the other two at the lower points of the pentagram to indicate the lambda.

4. Place two carnelian crystals just above and to either side of the tiger's eye in the center.
5. Place the remaining three carnelians below the center tiger's eye, two to each side and one slightly below. The five carnelian crystals should form the points of an inverted pentagon.
6. The combination of the lambda, the pentagon, and the pentagram will give your altar a protective shield. Keep the shield up for as long as it serves you. When it is time to disassemble the matrix, you can keep a few of the crystals with you when you are in need of protection.

CRYSTAL LATTICE FOR SPIRITUAL ASCENSION

Creating a crystal matrix is a meditative act. No matter what your intention or purpose, the mindfulness of deliberate placement can create a sense of calm and peace that will allow you better opportunities to develop your psychic gifts as a witch. It is difficult to see beyond or reach beyond when your mind is cluttered with distractions. Creating the ascension matrix is a form of not only spiritual connection but also basic self-care. It gives you the chance to engage with higher planes, explore the patterns that govern the universe, and take time for yourself for peaceful contemplation as a foundation for elevating your practice. This configuration is based on the Fruit of Life, which represents the sacred pattern within the Flower of Life.

Crystal Lattice for Spiritual Ascension

All of the crystals in this lattice have been chosen for their metaphysical associations as well as their ability to harmonize with and amplify each other, making this a particularly powerful crystal matrix.

You Will Need

- Identity crystal, either your birthstone, your zodiac stone, or your favorite crystal

- 13 rough or tumbled crystals. Select from the following list:
  - Amethyst
  - Apophyllite
  - Celestite
  - Chrysoberyl
  - Fluorite
  - Golden beryl (heliodor) or golden feldspar (golden healer)
  - Moonstone
  - Clear quartz
  - Selenite
  - Sunstone
  - Topaz
  - Turquoise
- 12 clear quartz or amethyst points (optional)

LATTICE *for* SPIRITUAL ASCENSION

1. Identity Crystal
2. Quartz
3. Sunstone
4. Golden Beryl
5. Apophyllite
6. Moonstone
7. Selenite
8. Topaz
9. Celestite
10. Amethyst
11. Flourite
12. Chrysoberyl
13. Turquoise

Directions

1. Place your identity crystal in the center of your altar.
2. Encircle it with six crystals from the list, using color as your guide. Create the circle with intention using the warm colors.
3. Create an outer circle with the remaining six crystals using the cool colors. *Optional:* Place crystal points in between the rough or tumbled crystals.
4. Once you have assembled the matrix, use it as a focal point of your meditation. Keep your eyes on the pattern, the colors, and the arrangement, and contemplate the power of a deliberate arrangement, your role as a creative force and creator of the matrix, and this expression of divine spirit capable of shifting reality.

The Power of the Matrix

This crystal matrix is considered to be a sacred arrangement reflected in the natural world and in heaven above. Creating the matrix gives you an expressive outlet with which to engage with higher powers. Meditating on the matrix strengthens your commitment to spiritual expression. Understanding your place in the matrix is calming, protective, and empowering, bringing you to a state of balance from which you can ascend into higher consciousness.

COSMIC HARMONY CRYSTAL SPELL

In order to align with the cosmos, it is important to acknowledge the proportional relationship between the earth and the moon. Witches use both the earth and the moon as significant sources of power in rituals, spells, and rites of passage. Witches also draw down the energy of the moon as part of sacred rituals. Here is a crystal matrix that you can build with the intention to strengthen your cosmic connection. This will deepen your abilities to work with these energies simultaneously. Use a crystal matrix combined with a spell to interact with the harmonious relationship between the moon, the earth, and yourself.

Cosmic Harmony Crystal Spell

For this spell you will need to choose ten crystals based on your needs. For example, if your spell intention is to balance responsibilities and communicate more clearly, you will choose a selection of iolite, sodalite, lapis lazuli, and clear quartz. If your intention is to strengthen a loving relationship, you will use peridot, aquamarine, and rose quartz. If you want to set your intention for prosperity and business success, you will use an assortment of pyrite, citrine, and aventurine. And if you want to protect your home, you will use smoky quartz, jasper, obsidian, hematite, and onyx.

You Will Need

- Matrix placement chart
- 10 crystals chosen according to your needs

MATRIX PLACEMENT CHART

Directions

1. Clear your altar space and clean and clear your crystals.
2. You will use the crystals to create the matrix representing the earth, the moon, and the Great Pyramid that will serve as the connection point between you and the cosmos.
3. Choose a crystal to represent you and your desired change. Place this crystal in the center of your altar.
4. Choose four crystals that represent what you need to manifest on earth. What will your desired change look like? How will your current situation be affected by the energy that you are calling in? Create a vision of your intention being actualized and place these four crystals equidistant above and below and to either side of the center point.
5. Place the next four crystals at the corners equidistant from above and below to frame the earth. This action protects and grounds your intention because the square you are creating has the same perimeter as the circle that will pass through the center of the final crystal.
6. The last crystal represents the moon, the source of power that you will draw from in order to manifest your desired situation. Place this crystal just above the crystal that aligns vertically with the center point.
7. Contemplate the relationship between the moon and the earth and the pyramid that joins them. Know that you are a part of this cosmic pattern and that your awareness of it can strengthen your magick, provide you with focus, and aid your ability to call things into being.

CRYSTAL HOME PROTECTION SPELL

Crystals can be powerful protective wards that can lend a feeling of comfort and security to your home. By placing crystals strategically around your home, you will have a stronger sense of well-being knowing that you have invested psychic energy into keeping your home protected against unwelcome visitors, disturbances, or disruptions to your peace and tranquility.

Crystal Home Protection Spell

You Will Need

- Black tourmaline
- Obsidian
- Jasper
- Smoky quartz
- Citrine

Directions

1. **Place the black tourmaline at your property boundaries.**
   These are the delineations that you want to control. Think of the tourmaline as a psychic boundary that you are linked with. Only you can decide who has the right to cross that boundary.
2. **Place the obsidian at your front entryway.**
   The obsidian is dark and opaque with a reflective surface. This will deflect any unwanted energy back to its source and away from your home. You may place it over a pediment or hang it from the doorknob.
3. **Place the jasper in the rooms where people are likely to gather.**
   These rooms can be the living room, study, and den; have the jasper visible on a mantel, shelf, or desk. Jasper has a grounding energy and will help minimize disputes and violations of personal boundaries pertaining to physical space. There are several varieties of jasper, making this an excellent crystal for grounding family energy.
4. **Place the smoky quartz on bedroom windowsills.**
   Smoky quartz also has grounding energy but of a more individual nature. Placing it on bedroom windowsills will promote peace and restful sleep.

5. **Place the citrine in the kitchen.**
   Citrine placed in the kitchen will promote happiness and cooperation. Citrine is also a stone of abundance, so keeping it in the kitchen will remind everyone that many hands make light work and that warmth and happiness and fulfillment are the dominant energies of the home.
6. If you wish, you can speak a charm to protect your home as you place the crystals. For example:

   May this house be blessed and protected by the ancient energy of the earth.
   May the gifts of the earth serve as symbols that we are provided for, protected, and committed to living in peace.
   May blessings flow through our door.
   So mote it be.

LIST OF WORKS CITED

"Amazonite." *Mindat.org*. www.mindat.org/min-184.html. Accessed 12/05/22.

"Amazonite." *National Museum of Natural History*. https://naturalhistory.si.edu/explore/collections/geogallery/10002689. Accessed 12.05.22.

American Gem Society. www.americangemsociety.org. Accessed 12/05/22.

American Gem Trade Association. https://agta.org/. Accessed 02/02/23.

Bancroft, Peter. *The World's Finest Minerals and Crystals*. New York: Viking Press, 1973.

Bell, Jim. *The Earth Book: From the Beginning to the End of Our Planet, 250 Milestones in the History of Earth Science*. New York: Sterling, 2019.

Birren, Faber. *Color Psychology and Color Therapy: A Factual Study of the Influence of Color on Human Life*. New York: Pickle Partners Publishing, 1961.

Bolton, H. Carrington. "A Modern Oracle and Its Prototypes. A Study in Catoptromancy." *The Journal of American Folklore* 6 (20), 1893: 25–37. https://doi.org/10.2307/534275. Accessed 2.02.23.

Bostock, John, and H.T. Riley, trans. 1855. *The Natural History of Pliny*, Vol II. York Street, Covent Garden, London: Henry G. Bohn.

Crosby, Tim. "Researcher Uncovers Oldest Amber Ever Recorded." *Southern Illinois University News*. https://news.siu.edu/2009/10/100209tjc9084.php. Accessed 01/04/23.

Evans, James. "The Astrologer's Apparatus: A Picture of Professional Practice in Greco-Roman Egypt." *Journal for the History of Astronomy* 35 (1), 2004: 1–44. https://doi.org/10.1177/002182860403500101. Accessed 1.29.23.

Frazer, Sir James George. *The Golden Bough: A Study in Comparative Religion*. London: Macmillan and Company, 1890.

GIA. www.gia.edu. Accessed 12/05/22.

Gordon, Susan. "Imagery and Symbolism in the Therapeutic Process." *Saybrook University*. www.saybrook.edu/2015/05/18/05-18-15. Accessed 12.05.22.

Gu, Ming Dong. "Divination and Correlative Thinking: Origins of an Aesthetic in the *Book of Changes and Book of Songs.*" *Philosophy and Literature* 46, no. 1 (2022): 120–136.

Kunz, George Frederick. *The Curious Lore of Precious Stones.* New York: Dover Publications, 1971.

Lee, M.R., Lindgren, P. "4.6-Billion-Year-Old Aragonite and Its Implications for Understanding the Geological Record of Ca-carbonate." *Carbonates and Evaporites* 30, 2015: 477–481. https://doi.org/10.1007/s13146-015-0257-2. Accessed 01/03/23.

Lichtenfeld, Stephanie, Andrew J. Elliot, Markus A. Maier, and Reinhard Pekrun. "Fertile Green: Green Facilitates Creative Performance." *Personality and Social Psychology Bulletin* 38(6), 2012: 784–797. https://doi.org/10.1177/0146167212436611. Accessed 12/19/22.

Lieben, John Oscar. *Sacred Geometry for Artists, Dreamers, and Philosophers: Secrets of Harmonic Creation.* Rochester, Vermont: Inner Traditions, 2018.

Nielsen, Arya. *Gua Sha: A Traditional Technique for Modern Practice.* Edinburgh: Elsevier Ltd., 2013.

https://sites.radford.edu/~jtso/GeoIVAHome.html. Accessed 01/29/23.

Roycroft, Patrick D., and Martine Cuypers. "The Etymology of the Mineral Name 'Apatite': A Clarification." *Irish Journal of Earth Sciences* 33, 2015: 71–75. https://doi.org/10.3318/ijes.2015.33.71. Accessed 11/12/22.

Taussig, Michael. "Tactility and Distraction." *Cultural Anthropology* 6(2), 1991: 147–153. www.jstor.org/stable/656411.

"The Power of the Placebo Effect." *Harvard Health Publishing.* www.health.harvard.edu/mental-health/the-power-of-the-placebo-effect. Accessed 11/26/22.

Tylor, Sir Edward Burnett. *Primitive Culture: The Origins of Culture.* Albemarle St., London: John Murray, 1920.

Verrill, A. Hyatt. *Precious Stones and Their Stories—An Article on the History of Gemstones.* Orchard Press, 2014.

INDEX

Note: Page numbers in **bold** indicate quick-reference facts of crystals. Page numbers in parentheses indicate intermittent references.

ABOUT THE AUTHOR

Judy Ann Nock, MS, is the bestselling author of seven books on witchcraft, including *The Modern Witchcraft Guide to Runes*, *The Modern Witchcraft Guide to Magickal Herbs*, and *The Modern Witchcraft Book of Natural Magick*. Her books have been translated into multiple languages and are enjoyed throughout the world. Judy Ann is a popular musician in Ivan Julian & the Magnificent Six, as well as the Hoboken supergroup Psych-O-Positive. She is an accomplished metalsmith, a graduate of the Gemological Institute of America, and a member of Mensa, and has appeared in *The New York Times*, *Publishers Weekly*, *The Guardian*, *Refinery29*, and *The Village Voice*. She lives with her daughter, Jaime, and her cat, Annabelle, in New York City.